THE POOL OF STARS

BY

CORNELIA MEIGS

CORNELIA MEIGS

CHAPTER I

THE DUSKY ROBBER

Elizabeth Houghton sat on a big stone beside the road, just where the highway forked, her school books still tucked under her arm. Her round blue eyes stared straight before her, as she tried, with one last effort, to make up her mind. For a whole week she had been attempting to reach a decision: that very morning she had told herself sternly that the matter must be settled to-day, yet still she had kept on debating inwardly, hour after hour, saying, one moment, "I will," and the next, "I won't." In the late afternoon she had set out for Aunt Susan's to announce her decision, but here she was pausing at the turn of the way, still irresolute.

If she went onward by the broad highroad that stretched before her, she would come to the big country-house where her aunt lived and where, once inside the door, all her doubts and hesitations would be swept away by Aunt Susan's forcible arguments. On the other hand, if she climbed the hill up the narrower branch of the way, Somerset Lane, she would come, she knew, to the white cottage beside the road where lived Miss Miranda Reynolds, a friend of her father's whom she had been bidden to go to see. When she set forth after school she had purposed vaguely going to one place or the other. If to Miss Reynolds', it would be putting off the moment of her decision a little longer, if to Aunt Susan's, it would end in settling the matter once for all.

She turned about on the stone and looked up the crooked path of Somerset Lane, winding steeply up the slope above her and ending before a great stone entrance-way with barred iron gates. Beyond the gates she could catch further glimpses of rising ground, groups of trees and, at the very summit of the hill, the broken walls of a ruined building. It must have been a fire, she concluded, after staring upward for some minutes, that had so blackened the stone walls and left them standing, empty and desolate, with here and there a blank window or the part of an arched doorway. For very weariness with pondering her own problem, she began to let her mind wander away in vague curiosity as to how such destruction had come about and how the fire had looked as it had swept blazing across the long roofs until they crashed and fell, had glowed behind the empty windows and had gone up in columns of sparks and flame above the dark trees. Her father had told her nothing of this big the top of the hill, he had merely directed her to look for cottage half way up the slope among the maple trees. No th thought, Miss Reynolds could give her an account of the gave some point to a visit in which she had felt very little interest now. She had a twinge of conscience as she sat looking up the lane remembering how long it was since she had promised her father to go, and how she should have climbed that steep way many days before.

Elizabeth had not lived very long in this neighborhood, for this was early spring and it had been only at Christmas time that she and her father and Irish Anna, who kept house for them, had come to Harwood to settle down in what had been Mr. Houghton's old home. Even here, after many other moves, the question of uprooting soon came up again, for in March her father had been summoned to England to spend six months.

"I wish it were not going to be so lonely for you, Betsey," he had said as he made preparations to go, "but at least you will be busy. I am glad that we have found such a good school for you at last. A few more changes, and your education would have been wrecked entirely."

Betsey had always meant to go to college and was now in the last half-year of her preparation. Transfers from one school to another had indeed resulted in so much lost time that she was already a little behind her proper class and would, so she agreed with her father, lose all chances of fulfilling her plans should she change again. She sighed deeply as she thought of it, sitting there upon the stone, for it was this very question that was casting shadows over a very brilliant prospect.

Very soon after Mr. Houghton's departure, Betsey's Aunt Susan, growing weary of the life of her quiet country place, big and luxurious though it was, had pressed upon her niece a dazzling invitation. It was to accompany her on a journey that would include Bermuda, Panama, California, and, when hot weather came, the Canadian Rockies. It became difficult for Elizabeth even to think of more months of plodding study, when, sitting at her desk, she could picture the flowers and palms of Bermuda, its coral caves with floors of rippling water, or the lazy breakers tumbling in on some California beach. But to go would mean giving up college, that was certain. And Elizabeth's mother, who had died five years before, had always wanted her to go to college!

So long did she sit there on the stone under the big oak tree, hesitating and debating, that presently there was a rumble of thunder, followed by the sharp spatter of rain on the little new leaves above her head. The low-hanging branches sheltered her like a roof so that she had only to sit there with her hands clasped about her knee, waiting for the shower to pass and for her puzzled thoughts to set themselves in order. She was wishing greatly for her father's advice, but that it would be impossible to get in time. Anna, good-natured and interested as she was, could offer little more than, "Sure it would be grand to go to college and learn so much," or, if the talk happened to turn in another direction, "Sure it would be grand to go to California and see all the pretty flowers," so that her opinions were of no very great help.

Elizabeth could see below her, as she sat there, rolling stretches of field and meadow and patches of woodland turning from brown to fresh spring green. Almost too far away to be visible on this day of fitful lights and shadows, were the crowded roofs and spires of a distant town and, to the east of them, the high, gray towers of that very college about which her dreams and ambitions had clustered so long.

"But it will be so lonely here!" she cried almost aloud, all her thoughts rising to sudden protest. She had friends of her own age at school, plenty of them, but what older person was there to whom she could go in doubt or difficulty, who was there to give her help or advice when she should need it? She felt lost and helpless at the thought and utterly forlorn. No, she could not bear it, she would go with Aunt Susan, her choice would be for change and travel and the seeing of beautiful things instead of the long empty road of hard work that stretched before her. Her battered geometry and Latin books slipped from her knee and lay, face downward and unheeded, on the grass. She had made up her mind—almost.

The shower had cleared and the clouds were sweeping away in rolling thunderheads of gray and shining silver. The moving sunlight touched the roofs of the town and lit, at last, the slim towers of the college so that they showed white and glittering against the dark background of the trees. Usually they seemed dim and distant, Elizabeth had thought, and never, as to-day, so near, so clear, possessed of such dignity of grace and beauty. She could not quite tell what it was, curiosity, doubt, hesitation, or all three at once that made her, when she got up to go, turn into Somerset Lane instead of along the highway, and that caused her to put off again the moment of letting Aunt Susan convince her that she should go to Bermuda.

She began to feel, as she climbed the hill, a good deal of curiosity concerning this Miss Miranda of whom her father had said so much and whom she should have gone to see long ago. Would she be all stiff manners and critical eyes, she wondered, the kind of person to make you feel awkward and tongue-tied the moment you crossed the threshold? It was the feeling that she must be something of the sort that had kept Betsey from coming for all this time. For some distance the lane wound and twisted so that she could not catch any glimpse of the white cottage that she sought. Once she stopped where a side path, a mere rough track bordered by Lombardy poplars, led away to the left. Could that be the way, she wondered, but no, it must lead only to the fields beyond, for here was a heavy white farm horse, evidently just come from plowing, turning into the path through a gap in the hedge. The big creature lifted his feet slowly, seeming comfortably tired after a well-spent day among the furrows, as he trudged leisurely along under the slender shadows of the wet poplar trees. He bore an equally weary rider, a boy of about Elizabeth's own age, who was perched sideways on the broad back, his legs swinging with every lurch of the horse's shoulders, his hat held on his knee so that Elizabeth could see plainly his hot, sunburned face and his rumpled, red-brown hair. He did not observe her, for he was looking away across the valley toward that same group of towers that she herself had been watching, as though the distant college held a fascination for him as well as for her. She thought for a moment of waiting to ask him the way, but her eye caught sight, just then, of a green roof above her among the trees and she went onward.

As she opened the gate beside the lane and walked up the path to the house, she felt, almost in spite of herself, an immediate liking for the place. It was a tiny white cottage with a wide-eaved roof, with two big red brick chimneys that told of broad hearthstones inside, with swinging windows and clambering vines and a square lawn skirted at one side by a high stone wall. Beyond this wall she could see again the blackened ruins that had aroused her curiosity as she sat at the crossroads below. What a wide and stately house it must have been there at the top of the hill and how strange it was that it had never been rebuilt! She must be sure to ask Miss Reynolds about it, for there was, somehow, a spell of haunting mystery about those roofless walls and empty windows that seemed to stare away across the wide view spread out below them. There was time for her to observe all these things as she stood upon the doorstep for, although she rang the bell twice, no one came to admit her.

"I don't want to come all this way for nothing," she thought; "I will go to the side door and find some way of leaving word that I have been here."

Following the pathway of flagstones, she turned the corner of the house and found that a wing of the cottage extended at right angles before her and that in it was a door, standing open. She stopped a moment to examine some crocuses that were pushing up through the new grass, but she was interrupted and startled by the sound of some one speaking, apparently to her.

"Good morning," a voice was saying, a harsh rough voice with a rasp and a squeak in it such as she had never before heard. "Good morning, good morning!"

She looked about, but could see no one. Evidently the sound came from within the open door, so she ran to it quickly and peeped inside.

A white-haired man sat at a table with his back to her, so intent upon what he was doing that it could not have been he who had spoken. She had expected to see a kitchen, but found instead that the place was some sort of a workshop with strange intricate pieces of machinery standing, some of them under glass cases, on benches and shelves along the walls. The man must be Miss Miranda's father, she concluded. She had heard her own father speak of him as quite a famous person, a scientist of long standing reputation. Yet it seemed a tiny, shabby place in which to find a great man! As she stood, wondering, upon the step, there came a hoarse chuckling from the shadows in the corner of the room and out came strutting and fluttering a big, black crow. He was not trying to talk now, but was cawing softly and clucking to himself as he advanced sideways, half spreading his wings and cocking his eye, first at the old gentleman, then at Betsey standing in the doorway. He had evidently some plot brewing in his wicked black head, for he fluttered to the edge of the table, sidled nearer and nearer and finally, with a sudden dart, pounced upon a pair of spectacles that lay on the blotter and flew out of the door over Elizabeth's head.

The old gentleman looked up, startled and blinking.

"Miranda, oh Miranda," he called helplessly. "That wretched Dick has stolen my spectacles again!"

Miss Miranda came running in from what must have been the kitchen, for she wore a blue apron and had a measuring cup still in her hand. Elizabeth saw at a glance that she was very pretty, with brown hair that curled and crinkled in spite of a streak or two of gray, and with cheeks that were pink from the heat of the fire.

"And I believe, my dear," her father added vaguely, as she came in, "that there is some one at the door."

It was astonishing to see what a strange effect this simple statement had, for Miss Miranda's face turned suddenly white and she looked toward the door with startled, frightened eyes. Her smile, when she saw who it was, seemed as bright with relief as it was with welcome.

"I think your crow has carried the spectacles up into that apple tree," announced Elizabeth, who had been watching the black thief and now saw him rocking on a high bough, cawing his triumph. "I can climb up and get them for you."

She dropped her school books on the step and ran across the grass quite forgetting to explain who she was or why she had come.

The branches of the tree were so low that the climb was no difficult one for a person as agile as Betsey. The wicked Dick fluttered about her head, rasping out his harsh protests, as she clambered higher and higher, but he had wedged his prize so firmly in a crotch that he could not get it out and was forced to see her carry it away. He was too well-trained a pet to attempt to peck her, but he sat on the wall and voiced his loud displeasure long after she had disappeared into the house.

The old gentleman put on the spectacles and returned to his work very placidly, as though such robberies were too frequent for comment. Miss Miranda led Elizabeth away toward her own little sitting room above her father's workshop.

"Won't you tell me about that house," Betsey began promptly, afraid that she might miss obtaining the information that she desired, "that place there beyond the wall that looks as if a fire—"

The glass cup that Miss Miranda still carried dropped clattering to the floor and shivered into a dozen pieces with a startling crash.

"How very awkward of me," she exclaimed apologetically as she stooped to gather up the fragments. Betsey, however, as she helped to collect the broken glass, had a vague realization that the awkwardness may have lain in her own blunt question and followed her new friend upstairs with no effort to follow her inquiries farther.

"There is another shower coming up," Miss Miranda said, "so we will light the fire here and be very cozy until it passes. I have just baked some gingerbread and some one really must try it while it is still fresh."

It was certainly delightful to sit in a cushioned chair by the wide fireplace where a few sticks were burning, to drink cool milk and eat new gingerbread and to hear the rain drumming on the tiles outside the casement window. Miss Miranda, sitting opposite with her knitting, was asking questions about Elizabeth's father, about her work and her school and her plans for college, in which she seemed to be much interested. But she did not force the talk and left her guest leisure to lean back in her chair, sip her milk and watch, through the rain-spattered glass, a wet robin taking refuge from the rain below the dormer window ledge.

"Yes," Betsey assented, in answer to one of the last questions, "I like the school work well enough, but sometimes it seems very long and hard and I cannot help thinking about—other things. I begin to believe these last months of the term will never end."

Miss Miranda had risen to fetch another ball of yarn and was standing now by the big mahogany secretary beyond the fireplace. Elizabeth was just beginning to notice what a wonderful old piece of furniture it was, so large that it occupied almost all of one side of the room. It had brass-handled drawers below and, above, glass doors that opened upon a perfect labyrinth of shelves, recesses and deep pigeonholes. She caught sight of something glittering on the topmost shelf.

"Oh, please, could I see what that is?" she begged. "The little tree—and oh, that silver figure just below. I never saw anything quite like them before."

Most willingly Miss Miranda threw both the doors wide open.

"This is the family toy-cupboard," she said. "The desk itself belonged to my great-grandfather, who was an officer in the Navy, and who used it to hold such treasures as he brought home from beyond the seas. Since his time every one of us who has something precious that he wants to keep or that has a story connected with it, puts it on these shelves. Many things have found their way here that I love dearly."

She set upon the table a row of strangely fashioned objects, a gold lacquer box with a trail of white wistaria across its lid, a big silver bowl with Moorish carvings, a long steel dagger with a thin blade and a twisted handle—a bewildering number of odd and beautiful treasures. It was over the last one that Betsey exclaimed aloud in delight. It was a little pine tree in a pot, twisted and gnarled and crooked, such as grows in Japanese or Chinese gardens, the whole not more than six inches high. At first she thought it was real and growing, but, on looking closer, saw that it was made of carved jade and enamel, set in a pot of gleaming yellow and white porcelain.

"Oh, where was it ever found?" she asked. "Who could have made anything so little and so lovely?"

Miss Miranda nodded, smiling.

"That is my favorite too," she said. "Would you think that human fingers, and they were old, stiff ones at that, could have carved anything so tiny as those perfect little needles and the brown cones? It was one of my great-grandfather's treasures; there are many things of his here, all of them a hundred years old. But here are some that are newer and this, the newest of all, is a silver medal my brother sent me from France, from the Jeanne d'Arc church in Domremy. He went overseas at the beginning of the war and, even now that it is over, still finds work to keep him, so that we do not know when he will come home. This silver figure that you asked about belongs to him, it is an image of Saint Christopher. An Irishman, Michael Martin, whom my brother Ted first knew when he visited some cousins in Montana and whom he afterward persuaded my father to bring here to work for us, gave him the little statue. Michael said that Ted was bound to be a wanderer and that Saint Christopher is especially good to travelers, that he keeps them from dangers by fire, storm, earthquake and such perilous things. But Ted, to Michael's great grief, never pays much attention to charms, and left Saint Christopher behind when he went to France, so I put it here for safe keeping in the toy cupboard."

Elizabeth was turning the little, shining figure over and over in her hand.

"It must have been Michael's most precious treasure," Miss Miranda went on. "He loved my brother so dearly that he wanted to give him the best he had. He is very old now and lives in a little house down the lane. He helps me with the garden still and is the most faithful and devoted friend that ever a family knew. I believe I must tell you how Ted first came to know him and of the adventure they had together that resulted in the coming of Michael and Saint Christopher into our household."

Elizabeth drew a deep sigh of satisfaction and settled down more comfortably among the cushions. Miss Miranda stirred the fire a little and took up her knitting.

"It all happened a great many years ago," she said, "but like all real stories it has not ended yet, nor will it until, as Michael claims, the spell of Saint Christopher brings my brother safe home again."

CHAPTER II

THE WHITE DOGS OF ARRAN

For a long hour, on that November afternoon, my brother Ted had been standing at the gate below the ranch house, waiting and waiting, while the twilight filled the round hollow of the valley as water slowly fills a cup. At last the figure of a rider, silhouetted against the rose-colored sky, came into view along the crest of the rocky ridge. The little cow pony was loping as swiftly as the rough trail would permit, but to Ted's impatient eyes it seemed to crawl as slowly as a fly on a window pane. Although the horseman looked like a cow puncher, at that distance, with his slouch hat and big saddle, the eager boy knew that it was the district doctor making his far rounds over the range. A swift epidemic had been sweeping over Montana, passing from one ranch to another and leaving much illness and suffering behind. Ted's uncle and the cousin who was his own age had both been stricken two days before and it seemed that the doctor would never come.

"I'm glad you are here," he said as the doctor's pony, covered with foam and quivering with fatigue, passed through the open gate. "We have two patients for you."

The man nodded.

"Fever, I suppose," he commented, "and aching bones, and don't know what to make of themselves because they have never been sick before? I have seen a hundred such cases in the last few days. It is bad at all the ranches, but the sheep herders, off in their cabins by themselves, are hit particularly hard."

He slipped from the saddle and strode into the house, leaving Ted to take the tired pony around to the stables. It was very dark now and growing cold, but he felt warmed and comforted, somehow, since the doctor had come. He heard running feet behind him and felt a dog's nose, cold and wet, thrust into his hand. It was Pedro, the giant, six months' old wolf hound puppy, long legged and shaggy haired, the pride of Ted's life and the best beloved of all his possessions. The big dog followed his master into the stable and sat down, blinking solemnly in the circle of lantern light, while the boy was caring for the doctor's horse and bedding it down.

Ted's thoughts were very busy, now with his anxieties about his uncle, now racing out over the range to wonder how those in the stricken ranch houses and lonely cabins might be faring. There was the ranch on Arran Creek—people there were numerous enough to care for each other. It might be worse at Thompson's Crossing, and, oh how would it be with those shepherds who lived in tiny cottages here and there along the Big Basin, so far from neighbors that often for months they saw no other faces than the woolly vacant ones of their thousands of sheep.

There was one, a big, grizzled Irishman, whom Ted had seen only a few times. Nevertheless, he was one of his closest friends. They had met on a night when the boy was hunting, and he could remember still how they had lain together by the tiny camp fire, with the coyotes yelping in the distance, with the great plain stretching out into the dark, with the slender curl of smoke rising straight upward and the big stars seeming almost within reach of his hand in the thin air. The lonely Irishman had opened his heart to his new friend and had told him much of his own country, so unlike this big bare one, a dear green land where the tumbledown cottages and little fields were crowded together in such comforting comradeship.

"You could open your window of a summer night and give a call to the neighbors," he sighed, "and you needn't to have the voice of the giant Finn McCoul to make them hear. In this place a man could fall sick and die alone and no one be the wiser."

His reminiscences had wandered farther and farther until he began to tell the tales and legends familiar in his own countryside, stories of the "Little People" and of Ireland in ancient times. Of them all Ted remembered most clearly the story of the white greyhounds of the King of Connemara, upon which his friend had dwelt long, showing that in spite of its being a thousand years old, it was his favorite tale.

"Like those dogs on Arran Creek, they were perhaps," the Irishman said, "only sleeker of coat and swifter of foot, I'm thinking."

"But they couldn't be faster," Ted had objected. "The Arran dogs can catch coyotes and jack-rabbits and people have called those the quickest animals that run."

"Ah," returned the other with true Irish logic, "those Arran dogs are Russian, they tell me, and these I speak of were of Connemara, and what comes out of Ireland you may be sure, is faster and fairer than anything else on earth."

Against such reasoning Ted had judged it impossible to argue and had dropped into silence and finally into sleep with the voices of the coyotes and the legend of the lean, white Irish greyhounds still running like swift water through his dreams.

After that he had visited the lonely shepherd whenever he could find time to travel so far. Together they had hunted deer and trapped beaver in the foothills above the Big Basin or, when the sheep had to be moved to new pasture, had spent hours in earnest talk, plodding patiently in the dust after the slow-moving flock. The long habit of silence had taken deep hold upon the Irishman, but with Ted alone he seemed willing to speak freely. It was on one of these occasions that he had given the boy the image of Saint Christopher, "For," he said, "you are like to be a great roamer and a great traveler from the way you talk, and those who carry the good Saint Christopher with them, always travel safely."

Now, as Ted thought of illness and pestilence spreading across the thinly settled state, his first and keenest apprehension was for the safety of his friend. His work done, he went quickly back to the house where the doctor was already standing on the door-step again.

"They are not bad cases, either of them," he was saying to Ted's aunt. "If they have good care there is no danger, but if they don't—then Heaven help them, I can't."

Ted came close and pulled his sleeve.

"Tell me," he questioned quickly, "Michael Martin isn't sick, is he?"

"Michael Martin?" repeated the doctor. "A big Irishman in the cabin at the upper edge of Big Basin? Yes, he's down, sick as can be, poor fellow, with no one but a gray old collie dog, about the age of himself, I should think, to keep him company."

He turned back to give a few last directions.

"I suppose you are master of the house with your uncle laid up," he said to Ted again, "and I will have to apply to you to lend me a fresh horse so that I can go on."

"You're never going on to-night?" exclaimed Ted; "why, you have been riding for all you were worth, all day!"

"Yes, and all the night before," returned the doctor cheerfully, "but this is no time to spare horses or doctors. Good gracious, boy, what's that?"

For Pedro, tall and white in the dark, standing on his hind legs to insert an inquisitive puppy nose between the doctor's collar and his neck, was an unexpected and startling apparition.

"That's my dog," Ted explained proudly; "Jim McKenzie, over on Arran Creek, gave him to me; he has a lot of them, you know. Pedro is only half grown now, he is going to be a lot bigger when he is a year old. Yes, I'll bring you a horse right away, yours couldn't go another mile."

When, a few minutes later, the sound of hoofs came clattering up from the stables it seemed certain that there were more than four of them.

"What's this?" the doctor inquired, seeing a second horse with saddlebags and blanket roll strapped in place and observing Ted's boots and riding coat.

"My aunt and the girls will take care of Uncle," the boy replied, "so I am going out to see Michael Martin. You can tell me what to do for him as we ride up to the trail."

They could feel the sharp wind almost before they began climbing the ridge. So far, summer had lingered into November, but the weather was plainly changing now and there had been reports of heavy snowfalls in the mountains. The stars shone dimly, as though through a veil of mist.

"You had better push on as fast as you can," advised the doctor as they came to the parting of their ways. "When a man is as sick as Michael, whatever is to happen, comes quickly." His horse jumped and snorted. "There's that white puppy of yours again. What a ghost he is! He is rather big to take with you to a sick man's cabin."

Pedro had come dashing up the trail behind them, in spite of his having been ordered sternly to stay at home. At six months old the sense of obedience is not quite so great as it should be, and the love of going on an expedition is irresistible.

"It would take me forever to drive him home now," Ted admitted; "I will take him along to Jim McKenzie's and leave him there with his brothers. I can make Arran Creek by breakfast time and ought to get to Michael's not long after noon. Well, so long!"

The stars grew more dim and the wind keener as he rode on through the night. His pony cantered steadily with the easy rocking-horse motion that came near to lulling him to sleep. Pedro padded alongside, his long legs covering the miles with untiring energy. They stopped at midnight to drink from the stream they were crossing, to rest a little and to eat some lunch from the saddlebags. Then they pressed on once more, on and on, until gray and crimson began to show behind the mountains to the eastward, and the big white house of Arran at last came into sight.

Jim McKenzie's place was bigger than the ordinary ranch house, for there were gabled roofs showing through the group of trees, there were tall barns and a wide fenced paddock where lived the white Russian wolfhounds for which the Arran ranch was famous. A deep-voiced chorus of welcome was going up as Ted and Pedro came down the trail. The puppy responded joyfully and went bounding headlong to the foot of the slope to greet his brothers. It was a beautiful sight to see the band of great dogs, their coats like silver in the early morning light, romping together like a dozen kittens, pursuing each other in circles, checking, wheeling, rolling one another over, leaping back and forth over the low fences that divided the paddock, with the grace and free agility of deer. Early as it was, Jim McKenzie was walking down to the stables and stopped to greet Ted as, weary and dusty, he rode through the gate.

"Sure we'll keep Pedro," he said when he had heard the boy's errand. "Yes, we've a good many sick here; I'd have sent out on the range myself but there was nobody to spare. They tell me the herds of sheep are in terrible confusion, and most of the herders are down. Poor old Michael Martin, I hope you get there in time to help him. Turn your horse into the corral, we'll give you another to go on with. Now come in to breakfast."

Ted snatched a hurried meal, threw his saddle upon a fresh pony, and set off again. For a long distance he could hear the lamentations of Pedro protesting loudly at the paddock gate. The way, after he passed Arran Creek, led out into the flat country of the Big Basin with the sagebrush-dotted plain stretching far ahead. It seemed that he rode endlessly and arrived nowhere, so long was the way and so unchanging the landscape. Once, as he crossed a stream, a deer rose, stamping and snorting among the low bushes, and fled away toward the hills, seeming scarcely to touch the ground as it went. Later, something quick and silent and looking like a reddish-brown collie, leaped from the sagebrush and scudded across the trail almost under his horse's feet.

"A coyote, out in the open in daylight," he reflected, somewhat startled. "It must have been cold up in the mountains to make them so bold. That looks bad for the sheep."

It was disturbing also to see how many scattered sheep he was beginning to pass, little bands, solitary ewes with half-grown lambs trotting at their heels, adventurous yearlings straying farther and farther from their comrades. Once or twice he tried to drive them together, but owing to his haste and his inexperience with their preposterous ways, he had very little success.

"There is going to be bad weather, too," he observed as he saw the blue sky disappear beneath an overcast of gray. "I had better get on to Michael's as fast as I can."

He saw the little mud and log cabin at last, tucked away among some stunted trees near the shoulder of a low ridge. It looked deceivingly near, yet he rode and rode and could not reach it. White flakes were flying now, fitfully at first, then thicker and thicker until he could scarcely see. His growing misgivings gave place to greater and greater anxiety concerning his friend, while there ran through his mind again and again, the doctor's words, "Whatever is to happen, comes quickly."

It was past noon and had begun to seem as though he had been riding forever when he breasted the final slope at last, jumped from his horse, and thundered at the cabin door. The whine of a dog answered him within, and a faint voice, broken but still audible, told him that Michael was alive.

The cabin, so it seemed to him as he entered, was a good ten degrees colder than it was outside. Poor Michael, helpless and shivering on the bunk in the corner, looked like the shrunken ghost of the giant Irishman he had known before. Ted rekindled the fire, emptied his saddlebags, piled his extra blankets upon the bed and, with a skill bred of long practice in camp cookery, set about preparing a meal. Michael was so hoarse as to be almost unable to speak and so weak that his mind wandered in the midst of a sentence, yet all of his thoughts were on the care of his sheep.

"When I felt the sickness coming on me I tried to drive them in," he whispered, "but they broke and scattered and I fell beside the trail—they must get in—snow coming—"

In an hour his fever rose again, he tossed and muttered with only fleeting intervals of consciousness. Ted had found food and shelter for his horse in the sheep shed, and had settled down to his task of anxious watching. The snow fell faster and faster so that darkness came on by mid-afternoon. He had tried to drive the old collie dog out to herd in the sheep, but the poor creature would not leave its master and, even when pushed outside, remained whining beside the door.

"He couldn't do much anyway," sighed Ted as he let him in again. "How those coyotes yelp! I wish, after all, that I had brought Pedro."

Michael had heard the coyotes too and was striving feebly to rise from his bed.

"I must go out to them, my poor creatures," he gasped. "Those devil beasts will have them driven over the whole country before morning."

But he fell back, too weak to move farther, and was silent a long time. When he did speak it was almost aloud.

"With the cold and the snow, I'm thinking there will be worse things abroad this night than just the coyotes."

He lay very still while Ted sat beside him, beginning to feel sleepy and blinking at the firelight. Eleven o'clock, twelve, one, the slow hands of his watch pointed to the crawling hours. Michael was not asleep but he said nothing, he was listening too intently. It was after one and the boy might have been dozing, when the old man spoke again.

"Hark," he said.

For a moment Ted could hear nothing save the pat-pat of the snow against the window, but the collie dog bristled and growled as he lay upon the hearth and pricked his ears sharply. Then the boy heard it too, a faint cry and far off, not the sharp yelping of the coyotes, though that was ominous enough, but the long hungry howl of a timber wolf.

Tears of weakness and terror were running down the Irishman's face.

"My poor sheep, I must save them," he cried. "What's the value of a man's life alongside of the creatures that's trusted to him. Those murderers will have every one of them killed for me."

Ted jumped up quickly and bundled on his coat.

"Where's your rifle, Michael?" he asked. "I don't know much about sheep, but I will do what I can."

"The rifle?" returned Michael doubtfully. "Now, I had it on my shoulder the day I went out with the sickness on me, and it is in my mind that I did not bring it home again. But there is the little gun hanging on the nail; there's no more shells for it but there's two shots still left in the chamber."

The boy took down the rusty revolver and spun the cylinder with a practiced finger.

"Two shots is right," he said, "and you have no more shells? Well, two shots may scare a wolf."

If Michael had been in his proper senses, Ted very well knew, he would never have permitted without protest such an expedition as the boy was planning. As it was, however, he lay back in his bunk again, his mind wandering off once more into feverish dreams.

"If it was in the Old Country," he muttered, "the very Little People themselves would rise up to help a man in such a plight. You could be feeling the rush of their wings in the air and could hear the cry of the fairy hounds across the hills. America is a good country, but ah—it's not the same!"

Hoping to quiet him, Ted took the little Saint Christopher from his pocket and laid it in the sick man's hand. Then he finished strapping his big boots, opened the door and slipped out quietly. Michael scarcely noticed his going.

The snow had fallen without drifting much, nor was it yet very deep. He hurried down the slope, not quite knowing what he was to do, thinking that at least he would gather as many sheep as he could and drive them homeward. But there were no sheep to be found. Where so many had been scattered that afternoon there was now not one. The whole of the Big Basin seemed suddenly to have emptied of them. Presently, however, he found a broad trail of trampled snow which he followed, where it led along a tiny stream at the foot of the ridge. As he turned, he heard again that long, terrifying howl coming down the wind. The sheep, perverse enough to scatter to the four winds when their master sought to drive them in, had now, it seemed, gathered of their own will when so great a danger threatened. Ted came upon them at last, huddled together in a little ravine where the sparse undergrowth gave some shelter from the snow. He could just see them in the dim light, their gray compact bodies crowded close, their foolish black faces seeming to look up piteously to him for help. They were very quiet, although now and then they would shift a little, stamp, and move closer. The cry of the wolf was stilled at last, but not because the fierce marauder was not drawing nearer.

Yes, as he stood watching, there slipped a swift dark shape over the opposite edge of the hollow and flung itself upon a straggling ewe on the outskirts of the flock. It was followed by a second silent shadow, and a third. The poor sheep gave only one frantic bleat, then all was still again save for the sound of a hideous snapping and tearing, of a furious struggle muffled in the soft depths of the snow. Ted raised the revolver and took careful aim, he pulled the trigger, but no explosion followed. Michael's improvidence in letting his stock dwindle to only two cartridges might be counted upon also to have let those two be damp. Helplessly the boy spun the cylinder and snapped the hammer again and again, but to no purpose.

The sheep was down now, with one of the savage hunters standing over it, another tearing at its throat while the third was slipping along the edge of the flock selecting a fresh victim. Ted's weapon was useless, yet he must do something, he could not stand and see the whole herd destroyed before his eyes. Perhaps he could frighten them away as one could coyotes: he was so angry at this senseless, brutal slaughter that he lost all sense of prudence. He waved his arms up and down and shouted at the top of his lungs. He saw the creatures drop their prey and turn to look up at him. He ran along the slope, still shouting, then, of a sudden, stepped into an unexpected hollow, lost his balance and fell headlong. One of the wolves left the flock and came creeping swiftly toward him, its belly dragging in the snow.

His cry must have carried far in the quiet of the night for it was answered from a great way off. A deep voice broke the stillness and another, the call of coursing hounds who have winded their quarry but have not yet found its trail. And mingled with the barking chorus there rose high the joyful yelp of a puppy who seeks his beloved master.

Ted, slipping in the snow, struggled to his knees and called again and again. The stealthy, approaching shadow crept a yard nearer, then paused to lift a gray muzzle and sniff the air. The second wolf, with slobbering bloody jaws, turned to listen, the flock of sheep snorted and stamped in the snow. A minute passed, then another. The boy managed to get to his feet. Then across the edge of the hollow, white against the dark underbrush, he saw the dogs coming, a line of swift, leaping forms, huge, shaggy and beautiful, their great voices all giving tongue together. Down the slope they came like an avalanche, one only separating himself from the others for a moment to fling himself upon Ted, to lick his face in ecstatic greeting and to rub a cold nose against his cheek. That nimble puppy nose it was that had lifted the latch of a gate not too securely fastened, and so set the whole pack free. Then Pedro ran to join his brothers who were sweeping on to battle. Wolfhounds are taught to catch, not to kill their quarry, but the thirst for blood was in the hearts of the dogs of Arran that night. There was only a moment of struggle, a few choking cries, and the fight was over.

Day broke next morning, clear and bright, with the chinook blowing, the big warm wind that melts the snows and lays the white hills bare almost in an hour. Michael Martin, fallen into a proper sleep at last, woke suddenly and sat up in his bunk. He startled Ted, who, rather stiff and sore from his night's adventures, was kneeling by the fire preparing breakfast. The boy came quickly to his patient's side to inquire how he did.

"It's better I am in body," the Irishman answered; "indeed I begin to feel almost like a whole man again. But—" he shook his head sadly, "my poor wits, they're gone away entirely."

"What can you mean?" Ted demanded.

Michael sighed deeply.

"After you were gone last night," he answered, "even my wandering senses had an inkling of what a dangerous errand it was, and I got up from my bed and stumbled to the window to call you back. Yes, the sickness has made me daft entirely, for as sure as I live, I saw the white greyhounds of Connemara go over the hill. But daft or no—" he sniffed at the odor of frying bacon that rose from the hearth, "I am going to relish my breakfast this day. Eh, glory me, if there isn't another of the creatures now!"

For Pedro, once more applying a knowing muzzle to the clumsy latch, had pushed open the door and stood upon the step, wagging and apologetic, the morning sun shining behind him. Long-legged and awkward, he stepped over the threshold and came to the bedside to sniff inquisitively at the little silver image that lay on the blanket. Michael could never be persuaded to believe otherwise than that Saint Christopher had brought him.

CHAPTER III

DAVID

When Betsey went, two days later, along the hill road again she walked far more quickly and did not hesitate at the turning of the lane. She was on her way to Aunt Susan's to announce her determination and she felt, this time, neither irresolution nor reluctance. She went firmly up the graveled drive, asked the grave butler whether her aunt were at home, and, waiting in the big, impressive drawing room, even heard the approaching rustle of Aunt Susan's elaborate silk skirts without feeling her courage give way.

"I have made up my mind not to go."

She got it out quickly, almost before a word of greeting had passed. "My father wants me to go to college and my mother did, too. If I should leave my work now I feel sure I would not do what I have planned. So— so I must stay."

There was no need for her to say how much she wished for the journey. She felt, in fact, that it was wise to say as little as possible and to bend all her efforts to resisting the storm of arguments and protests that would be poured out upon her. Aunt Susan was a person much accustomed to having her own way and was dangerously skillful at persuading people to do her bidding.

"Think how lonely you will be," she began immediately.

Once this had been the single thought that made staying at home seem unendurable, but now even that difficulty, it seemed, could be faced. In one short afternoon at Miss Miranda's, Elizabeth had felt herself surrounded by such a warmth of friendliness that already she felt certain that here would be a refuge where she would be welcome and at home, no matter how empty and deserted her own house might seem. To come home from school, weary with the labors of the day and find no one there save Anna, busy in the kitchen and not wishing to be disturbed, to have no one glad to see her or desirous of knowing just how things had gone —it had seemed a depressing prospect. But now that she knew Miss Miranda it was somehow different. Elizabeth could not have explained just why she felt, after only an hour or two of acquaintance, after only a little talk, that here was a friend to stand by her through everything. Feel it she did, however, and with the knowledge, made firm her decision. But to hold to that decision was not so easy.

"I was absolutely certain that you would come with me," Aunt Susan exclaimed, trying a new point of attack. "I had even decided what clothes you were to have. Your traveling suit was to be green faille silk with white furs."

Betsey had before had experience with dresses planned by Aunt Susan. They were apt to be of the sort in which you could not run upstairs, or that split their sleeves if you raised your arms suddenly, but they were always very beautiful. She sighed a little at the thought of the white furs.

"And I dare say you could go to school here and there in places where we stopped long enough," her aunt went on; "that ought to be all you need for keeping up your work."

She had not been to college herself and had not grasped the fact that dropping in upon one school and then another could fail to produce all the education necessary. Elizabeth tried to explain, but found it useless. She wished that, having stated her determination, she could go home at once, for the longer she stayed the more irresistible and enticing did the journey seem. She had rashly consented to stay to dinner, however, and so must prepare for a long struggle. The dinner was half enjoyable on account of the beautiful things on the table, silver and flowers and frail china that Betsey loved, and half terrifying on account of the things that Aunt Susan might be going to say next. She said a great deal, she exclaimed, she expostulated, she persuaded, until her niece was at the point of exhaustion.

"But it will be so dreary, all by yourself!" she kept insisting, in answer to which Betsey continued to maintain stoutly—

"Miss Miranda is going to be a good friend to me. I will not be entirely alone."

"Do you mean Miranda Reynolds who lives on the hill, up Somerset Lane?" Aunt Susan inquired. "I am very fond of her myself, but somehow I never seem to see much of her nowadays. How do you happen to know her?"

"She came to see me, but I was a long time in going there to return her visit. I did not know how nice her house was, or how kind she would be, or what interesting things she would tell me."

"I do not suppose," returned Aunt Susan slowly, with a shade of curiosity in her voice, "that she told you how she happens to be living in a gardener's cottage and cooking and scrubbing and tending cabbages and ducks when she might be doing—oh, very different things?"

"No," answered Betsey, "no, she did not tell me that."

Now that she thought of it, there were a great many things that Miss Miranda had not told her. She knew very little of her new friend and, in spite of questionings among acquaintances of her own age, seemed unable to learn more. She had discovered only that Miss Miranda dwelt in the cottage alone with her father, that she had a big vegetable garden on the sunny slope of the hill, that she kept ducks and chickens and, by her untiring industry, managed to make the household prosper. Elizabeth could well believe that to whatever she turned her hand, that thing would be successful.

"Her father was quite a great man in his day," her aunt went on thoughtfully. "He had a good deal of a name as an expert in scientific mechanics. One never hears of him now. I suppose he does not accomplish much since he has grown old. I am continually thinking that I will go over to see Miranda, yet I have so many engagements that I never do. She sent me some delightful asparagus from her garden lately; I have meant to give her some of Simmonds' grapes in return. You can leave them there to-night when the motor takes you home. Yes, you will have a good friend in her, but you are very wrong and foolish not to go with me, just the same."

As Elizabeth, leaning back in the big car, rolled along the smooth road on her way home, she could not help wondering how it would be to have just such luxury at her command for the next few months, to travel in splendor with Aunt Susan and to see all the wonderful things of which she had just heard such dazzling description.

"It is not too late yet, if you want to change your mind," had been her aunt's last words. Betsey was nearer to wavering at this moment than ever before. The thought of the still, empty house to which she was coming home, seemed suddenly very dreary indeed.

The car stopped at the Reynolds' gate and Elizabeth went in herself with the basket of grapes. The curtains were not drawn, so that she could see Miss Miranda sitting with her work beside the table. She could even see her look up, startled and alarmed as she had been before, when there came a step at the door. She was so calm, so quiet and cheerful in all other matters it was hard to imagine why this one thing should trouble her so. After the basket was delivered, Elizabeth lingered at the door, unwilling to say good night, while Miss Miranda, too, seemed reluctant to have her go. When at last Betsey took her departure and the car moved away from the gate, she found that her wavering doubts, felt so keenly at Aunt Susan's, had vanished again. She would not be too lonely if she had Miss Miranda, of that she now felt doubly assured; but there was something more. She had an odd, protective feeling for her new friend, as though she were staying at home, not only to carry out her own plans, but to take care of Miss Miranda.

There is sometimes a vague knowledge of things that comes without words. It was clear enough to Elizabeth, long afterwards, just what heavy trouble was brooding over the little household of the cottage, and just what part she was destined to play in dispelling it. Yet it was curious indeed, that she should have begun to feel, so early and so distinctly, that here she was really needed and that here she would give, in return for Miss Miranda's friendship, not only small services but great ones.

The sunny garden on the hillside was being planted on the afternoon that she came to the cottage again. She had said good-by to Aunt Susan that morning and had seen her depart in a great flutter of veils and furs and feathers. The train had rolled away carrying with it Betsey's last vision of snow-capped mountains, sparkling blue seas, tropical shores and white, flower-crowned cliffs. Her mind would still linger, in spite of herself, on the pleasures that she had renounced so that she was glad to find some absorbing diversion and to turn her abundant energy to helping Miss Miranda.

The peas were already pushing their pert green noses through the warm soil, and the scattered lettuce plants showed all along the row. Betsey became so entranced with the task of setting out beans that she would have filled the whole garden with them had not Miss Miranda warned her that there must be a little space left for beets and carrots and sweet corn.

Old Michael Martin, bent and weatherbeaten, the hero of the tale she had heard on her first visit, was at work spading the far end of the garden. He seemed a silent, crabbed person, who did not like to answer even when spoken to, so that Betsey found him rather disappointing. He would stop his work now and then, however, to hurl a few words of rather bewildering advice at the two among the bean rows.

"If you are to plant lettuce again, Miss Miranda," he remarked suddenly, standing with both hands resting on his spade, "you had best be doing it to-day. It is the very last of the light of the moon."

"What does he mean?" inquired Elizabeth in an undertone when he had gone on with his work again. She had no notion that moonlight need be considered in the matter of growing vegetables.

"He thinks that everything in a garden goes by signs and wonders," Miss Miranda answered. "He says charms for luck when he puts in the cabbage plants, and he thinks that if the first peas are not sown on Saint Patrick's Day, they will none of them come up at all. It is high time to set out the onions to-day, but he would be so disturbed at putting them in before the dark of the moon that I have not the heart to insist on it. All crops that grow under ground, he claims, must be planted in the dark of the moon, and those that ripen above, some time between its waxing and waning. So to-day is the day for lettuce and next week he will plant potatoes and beets and carrots and after I have tended them like babies all summer he will nod wisely when they grow big and say, 'Oh, yes, of course they can't help flourishing if you plant the right things in the dark and the light of the moon.' But it does happen to be a good day for the lettuce. I am afraid that I have left the seeds on the kitchen table."

Elizabeth volunteered to get them, and went up the path from the garden, past the big pen where the ducks and chickens were, and where a dozen brown-yellow ducklings were waddling solemnly forth on their first expedition into the outside world. She stopped to drive them back and then went on, across the lawn, to the open door of the cottage.

When she first came up the lane that day, she had noticed that the same big white horse that she had seen in the poplar-bordered cart track was now plowing in the field opposite the Reynolds' cottage. It was guided by the same red-haired boy, who went plodding up and down the rows, leaving behind them a straight, blue-black ribbon of upturned soil. She stopped to watch for a moment as they came near the fence and she thought that he looked up and saw her, for she caught sight of a pair of very blue eyes and a fair, much-freckled face.

As she paused, however, there arose suddenly in the workshop wing of the cottage, such a wild crashing, such a commotion of whirring wheels and creaking machinery that she flew to the door to see what had happened. The crow's voice mingled with the din, upraised in caws of loud excitement, while finally, during a faint lull, Mr. Reynolds was also to be heard, calling in the familiar tone of worried helplessness—

"Miranda, oh, Miranda."

At first she could not make out what was happening, so full did the place seem to be of flapping black wings, whirling wheels and spinning pulleys. At last, however, she managed to understand that one of the big machines at the end of the shop was in violent motion and that a broken rod was flying round and round with the spinning wheel, smashing and crashing against everything that came in its way. Even in the midst of the noise Mr. Reynolds must have heard Elizabeth come in, for he glanced at her quickly over his shoulder.

"Climb up on that stool and throw the switch there above the workbench," he directed. "That is the only way to stop this thing and I can't leave the broken crank-shaft."

Even in her haste Betsey noticed how quiet and cool he was, and with what quick skill he was adjusting valves and closing cylinder cocks, all the time keeping out of the way of the plunging and slashing of the broken rod. The switch was so stiff that she tugged at it to no purpose; she jerked and struggled but without effect. Mr. Reynolds looked back at her anxiously as the whirring and crashing grew every moment more violent. She thought of Miss Miranda, but she was far away in the garden and perhaps would not have sufficient strength, nor would Michael. With sudden inspiration she jumped down and sped through the door and across the lawn. The boy and his white horse were just turning a furrow beside the fence, only the breadth of the road away.

"Come quickly," she called in unceremonious haste. "We need you."

The boy dropped his reins, left the horse standing in the furrow and vaulted over the fence. His face, his white shirt and his blue trousers were all coated alike with dust but she noted with satisfaction how broad his shoulders were and how quickly he moved. In one second he was at the door, in another seemed to know entirely what to do. The stiff handle groaned as he jerked the switch and flung it over to break the current, the wildly spinning wheels began to slow down and finally, imperceptibly, came to rest. The old man turned about to thank them, his gray eyes under heavy white brows, alight with high excitement.

"Did you have an accident?" Betsey inquired breathlessly. "I don't understand what happened. Are you hurt?"

"The rod caught me a crack across the knuckles when it first gave way, but it does not signify," he replied cheerily.

The boy had come nearer and was examining the machine with what seemed a practiced eye.

"It was a flaw in the steel, I suppose," he said. "But what is this machine? I never saw anything like it before."

Mr. Reynolds began explaining as fully as though the stranger were a fellow engineer, just how he was trying to perfect a new power engine that would run on less fuel than the old ones. "For," he said, "as there grows to be less and less of coal and oil in the world, men must be keeping their wits alive to improve mechanics and keep the wheels of industry turning." The boy became more and more interested, asking quick questions and receiving eager answers. Elizabeth began to feel a little left out as technical terms flew back and forth concerning things she did not understand. She stood soothing black Dick who, still excited, was talking to himself in a corner.

"I have tried a good many models," Mr. Reynolds was saying, "but this one is the newest and it developed so much more power than I expected, that it came near to tearing itself to pieces before you came to my rescue. If it had been wrecked I should have had to begin all over again at the beginning."

"I believe you should not have tried it when you were all alone," commented Betsey sagely. "You should have made sure that some one was within call."

The old man smiled, a gentle smile lit with the warmth of much affection.

"I thought it better to try it when Miranda was not in the house," he answered. "If it had refused to run I did not want any one to know of it.

My daughter is always very quick to see when I am disappointed, and I do not like to give her pain."

He took up a wrench to loosen a bolt but found it jammed and immovable. With ready skill the boy took the tool from him and unscrewed the obstinate nut.

"By the way," questioned the old man, "ought I to remember your name? Have I ever seen you before?"

His confessed absent-mindedness was so disarming that the boy laughed.

"Miss Miranda knows me," he said, "but you have never seen me, at least you have never noticed me. My name is David Warren, and I am staying with my uncle who owns the place on the east side of this hill. He is farming a great part of it this year and finds labor so difficult to get that I am working for him for the spring and summer. And I think old Dobbin will be wondering where I have gone and will be dragging his plow all across the field. You have a wonderful thing here, this machine. I—I would like to come and see it run again."

He was out of the door and across the road before a word could be said to thank him. Elizabeth, still feeling rather dazed with the suddenness of the whole affair, returned to her forgotten errand of fetching the lettuce seeds, which Miss Miranda would surely be needing by now. However, on coming back to the garden, she found that her long absence had been scarcely noticed. The brown ducklings had escaped again and even Michael had been obliged to put down his spade and go in pursuit of them.

"Shoo, ye varmints," he was saying, as the fat balls of down, their lemon-colored bills wide open in faint baby quackings, went scuttling in a dozen different directions from between his feet. "You might know they would be wild creatures, they were hatched out in a thunderstorm!"

The afternoon had been cheerful, but the evening was long and lonely, with Anna plunged into one of her blackest moods. Yet, though the hours dragged, they did not suffice for the mastering of to-morrow's lesson. Geometry and history were Betsey's two great difficulties, so great indeed that, with the college examinations coming nearer, they began vaguely to threaten real disaster. She sighed as she turned for the tenth time to the worn page in her textbook, dealing with the volume of the frustum of a pyramid. She knew the drawing and the text drearily by heart, but would she ever understand it? Would the looming bulk of this misshapen figure grow bigger and bigger until it blocked her road to higher education? As she crept away to bed she was thinking that it was only that morning that Aunt Susan had left her, proclaiming to the last Betsey's mistaken foolishness in remaining behind. Perhaps, after all, Aunt Susan had been right!

She awoke next morning still depressed, more discouraged than ever when her eye fell upon the cover of her geometry book. It would be a good plan to set off for school early, she decided, and go around by Somerset Lane for a cheering moment of talk with Miss Miranda. Her heart felt lighter as soon as she thought of it.

As she turned in at the gate her glance swept the field across the way, but found it empty. No sturdy white horse was plowing it to-day, no erect, copper-haired figure was visible, only rows of furrows, drying in the sun. The little house, also, seemed unusually quiet as she first rang at the bell, then went across the grass to knock at the kitchen door. She could hear Mr. Reynolds tinkering in the shop, she could see Michael's bent back where he was toiling alone in the garden. She saw, presently, when the door opened, the unattractive face of a totally strange woman who was apparently presiding over Miss Miranda's kitchen. In the fewest and shortest words possible the stranger explained to Betsey that Miss Miranda was gone.

"Gone? Gone where? For how long?" cried Elizabeth in unbearable disappointment.

But she received no answer for the woman had already closed the door.

CHAPTER IV

THE DOOR IN THE WALL

Spring had advanced to that season of damp, hot, sunny days and rainy nights when all things are growing at such speed that shrubs and trees are top-heavy with their new green shoots and are easily shaken by the wind, while people feel restless and uneasy and would like to be doing something different from the tasks before them. Elizabeth often found school dull and oppressive, with the air of the room close, with her feet shuffling beneath her desk from the long hours of quiet and with her thoughts wandering so far away that the page of her book was only a blur before her. Every day, when she walked home, she would make a detour up Somerset Lane just to look at the cottage, to notice how green the vegetable garden was growing, how the pea vines were tall enough to be swinging in the wind.

Once she came across Mr. Reynolds, strolling on the lawn for a breath of air, Dick perched in solemn state upon his shoulder. She questioned him at once as to Miss Miranda's term of absence and what her sudden departure might mean.

"I did not quite understand it myself," he answered, seeming to be as distressed as Betsey in his vague, absent-minded way. "She seemed to decide on going very much of a sudden, but—I do not quite know—it appears to me that she had been a little uneasy for some time, a little troubled when people came suddenly to the door. Well, well, perhaps the journey will quiet her."

He turned to go back to his shop. He did not invite Betsey to enter, probably, indeed, he had forgotten all about her the moment he crossed the doorstep.

There came Friday afternoon a month, it seemed, from the last Friday, when Miss Miranda had gone away. As Elizabeth walked along the lane, feeling the air hot and heavy with coming rain, she hesitated a moment at the turning, listening to the muttered thunder in the distance and knowing that a downpour was not far off. From the breathlessness of the whole world about her and the increasing blackness overhead, she realized that this was to be no such spring shower as had once delayed her on that same road, but a real and furious thunderstorm. Yet she could not refrain from turning up the hill, so anxious was she to know whether or not Miss Miranda had returned. She felt hopeful at least of getting, through Mr. Reynolds' vague answers to her questions, or from Michael's grunted yes or no, some information as to when the mistress of the house might be expected. There was no one in sight to-day, however, for the lawn was vacant, the garden empty and the windows closed and blank as though even Mr. Reynolds and the sour woman in the kitchen had deserted the place. She lingered at the gate, lonely and disappointed.

"I'll walk down through the garden and see how the onions and the ducks are getting on," she said to herself. "It's not going to rain so very soon."

She knew at heart that this was not true, that the tenseness of the air meant that the storm must break any moment, and that the boiling clouds just becoming visible over the edge of the hill contained thunder and lightning and a deluge of rain. Nevertheless she pressed on, anxious to be of service to her friend, thinking that there might be some young chickens to rescue or some wayward ducklings to drive in out of the storm. Reaching the gate of the poultry yard she found that the motherly old hens had been as thoughtful as she, for they had long since hustled their young charges under shelter, leaving only the old red cock to strut about the place and cast his eye upward at the threatening clouds. She was leaning over the gate, laughing at his absurd dignity, when the whole sky above her was streaked with a blinding flash of light and the very hill seemed to rock under the following thunder. The big drops began to fall, faster and faster, until a white sheet of rain swept across the garden almost before she could seek refuge in the open door of the tool shed.

How it poured, so that trickling streams were running down the paths and pools were collecting before her very feet! What was it doing to the garden laid out on the long slope, all that flood of water rushing from the top of the hill to the valley below? A good many times she had heard Michael comment to Miss Miranda on just such a possibility.

"'Tis a good bit of ground you have, but steeper by far than it should be. In grass it was well enough, but in garden stuff, I'm not so certain. A hard rain on this hillside would cut the rows and wash out the young plants something cruel. I wish it were more of a level."

Just what he had dreaded was evidently happening now. Rain and wind rushed furiously over the garden, flattening the peas, tearing at the furrows, plowing deep trenches where rivulets of water went streaming down. Once in a quieter shower she had seen Michael working with a hoe, opening proper channels to carry off the rain, making little ditches here and there where the water could flow away without doing harm. It was plain that if the garden was to be saved from the ravages of this seasonable storm, some such thing must be done now.

"Well," she thought determinedly, "I wasn't of much use in the workshop, but I can do something here at least."

It had rankled a little for some days after that other emergency, to remember that it was David and not herself, who had been of service.

She took a hoe from behind the door and ran out into the rain. In a moment her hat was blown away, her clothes were soaked and water was streaming down her face. She struggled valiantly with the torrents that were pouring through the garden. At first she was slow and awkward, but presently she gained skill by experiment so that she could open channels where they were most needed and could forestall the cutting of cruel gashes all across the rows of the best vegetables. Energy and good will she had in plenty and with abundance of these she toiled, wet, muddy, slipping in the crumbling soil, thinking sometimes that she was beaten but still fighting desperately to rescue what she could. At last slowly, very slowly, the struggle turned from a losing battle to a winning one, the proper ditches were made and maintained, the rain softened from a deluge to a quiet shower, the water flowed harmlessly away between the corn and the cabbages and Betsey stopped to draw breath and survey what she had done. The peas and onions showed unbroken rows, the beans had been little damaged, the bulk of the garden's crop had been saved. It was only then that she realized how excited she had been and how wet and weary she was. She jumped with startled suddenness when a voice spoke behind her.

"You've done that none so bad," it said slowly. "There's not many that's so willing to keep a garden from being ruined by the rain and fewer yet would have the wits to know how."

She turned to see Michael Martin sitting on an upturned bucket, smoking calmly away at his stump of a black pipe, rain dripping from the rim of his battered hat.

"I remembered seeing you carry off the rain in the same way last week," Betsey answered, "so I thought I'd try it myself. But I didn't know that you were anywhere near."

"That was but an April shower," he rejoined, "such as a stiff old man could get the better of, but I've known this long time that I wasn't able any more to fight one of these unseasonable thunderstorms. The ground here lies well for the sun but ill for the rain, as I'm always telling Miss Miranda. She'll be glad and thankful that you have saved her crop! And how it did rain, as though it were Saint Swithin's Day itself!"

"And how long have you been sitting there?" demanded Betsey. "You might at least have told me what to do."

"I came out thinking to try what I could myself, but when I saw you at the work, I could tell that you knew what you were about, so where was the use of wasting any words. I just waited in case you needed any help, but you managed better alone than with an old man to hinder. I've no doubt that your hands are blistered and that you'll find your back aching to-morrow, but you have saved the garden. It will be something Miss Reynolds will be glad to hear when she comes home."

"Is she coming soon? Where did she go?" Elizabeth inquired eagerly.

"Now that I don't know," Michael answered with a sigh. "She decided within an hour and off she went. It might have been to consult her cousin that looks after her business affairs and that used to live here when he was a boy."

"What was her cousin's name?"

The rain had almost ceased, so Elizabeth laid aside her hoe, stretched her cramped fingers and went to stand in front of Michael and ply him with questions. Such a talkative mood was so rare in him that she feared, any second, it might pass away, and, since here at last was some one who could and would tell her more of Miss Miranda, she trembled lest silence should come suddenly upon him before she had heard what she wished to know. The rain was pattering from her skirts, her feet sank every moment deeper into the mud, but she feared to move or turn away lest the spell should break. Good fortune seemed to be with her, however, for Michael talked on and on, relighting his pipe as often as the water quenched it, and answering her queries to the best of his ability.

"His name was Don, Mr. Donald Reynolds he is now, and I find it hard to remember when I see him, that they were ever little things here together and he was her Cousin Don. I never liked the lad, and began to mistrust him from the first I knew of him, when his face was just beginning to look keen and sharp and he was learning to think it was a great joke that he could so easily get the better of the other two, Miss Miranda and Mr. Ted, and shape things to go all his way. Now he is rich and prosperous and beginning to grow fat, but still he has that sharp, selfish face. He has forgotten how to be kind to Miss Miranda, he has forgotten how good she was to him when he was a snub-nosed boy with long legs and skinned knees and the both of them with no mother. Yes, he has forgotten all that, has Mr. Donald Reynolds."

"And you think she has gone somewhere to consult him?" Elizabeth asked.

"She goes to see him rarely, more often he comes here. And she dreads his coming always. I begin to know when it is time for another visit from him, when she starts at the creaking of the gate and begins to look frightened when she hears a step coming up the path. She has been in worse uneasiness than ever, these last weeks, so I'm thinking she just decided that it was better to dare than to dread, so she was off to see him and have it over."

"But why," persisted Betsey, "why should she be afraid of her own cousin when he grew up with her?"

"It's past my understanding," Michael admitted, "and I've thought and wondered over it until my mind was all at sea. I'm not of her kind, so it's a puzzle that I can't solve. It has something to do with her old father, and that machine he is making, that far I have got, but no farther. He is a clever one, the old man; he has been famous once and I'll wager you, when that piece of work is done, he will make the world talk of him again. But there's something wrong and if one but knew what it was, maybe it could be put right. When I knew them first they were all so happy, living there in the big house at the summit of the hill, they seemed to have everything in life there was to wish for, but since then the house has burned and Mr. Ted has gone away to the wars, and there's things gone badly awry. Miss Miranda doesn't pretend that this big garden and these ducks and hens are here for her own pleasure, she owns that she must have the money that she makes by them, but it's my belief that not even you and I know how much she needs it."

His damp pipe, rebellious at last, refused to be rekindled, which delayed him for a long minute.

"She has cut herself off from most of her old friends," he went on, when he was once more puffing vigorously, "for fear they might be asking questions or offering help in a way that would hurt her. She is too proud to endure either. But—" he raised his little gray eyes and looked at Betsey keenly, "but you're of a different sort, the sort that she does not fear and that can be a true friend to her none the less. She is fond of you, I've seen that in these days you have worked with her in the garden. Be good to her, Miss Betsey, and stay near to her. Find out her trouble if you can and help her. For it's as true as that there are Saints in Heaven, it's help she needs."

He got up as though all that he had been saying had led up to this and now he had finished.

"But—" gasped Betsey, "but, please tell me first—"

His square jaw shut so firmly that she knew there was no use in going on. The strange mood of fluent speech had left him. Pocketing his pipe and pulling his wet hat down over his forehead, he stumped off down the muddy furrow, never looking back. The rain had ceased entirely now and the sun had come breaking through the clouds with that brilliant clearness that often follows a storm. It made the drenched green rows glisten and the new corn, bowing before the wind, sparkle and drop jewels as the gusts passed by. Betsey slowly lifted one heavy foot out of the mud and then the other, and walked very thoughtfully up the path.

On Saturday and Sunday she went away into the country with some friends of her own age to stay at a distant country place and to spend the quick hours in very happy holiday-making, returning to school on Monday morning with more energy and cheerfulness than she had known for a week. Affairs of various kinds kept her occupied so late that it was not until the long daylight hour after dinner that she was free to hasten away up Somerset Lane. As she came to the gate she saw with delight that there were lights in the upper windows, that the doors stood open and that the whole place had a more cheerful look than it had recently worn. Even Dick, sitting on the gate post and conversing with himself in happy gutturals, seemed trying to announce that the mistress of the house was once more at home.

Miss Miranda said nothing of her journey except to thank Elizabeth most warmly and gratefully for saving the garden in her absence.

"You should hear Michael sing your praises," she said. "He has so little to say of any one that it is amazing to hear how he talks of you. He cannot make up his mind whether we have saved our season's crop through your resourcefulness or because last week he buried a luckpenny at the head of the garden. But I know what I think!"

They went out together to inspect the whole place, to wonder at the growth of the vegetables after the rain, and to admire the plumpness of the ducks and the white Leghorn chicks, hatched while Miss Miranda was away. Betsey noticed that her friend still looked worn and anxious and that the old trick of looking quickly over her shoulder when a step went past the gate, was not gone. But of her journey she still said nothing.

"I think," Miss Miranda remarked at last, "that it would be pleasant to walk over to the big house—or where the big house stood—and look at the flowers there. The peonies should be out by now. I was thinking of them to-day, of how cool and white they were and what banks of them should be blooming under the dining-room windows. The air feels close to-night, but there is nearly always a breeze stirring under the pine trees across the slope of the hill."

The high gray wall that edged the lawn by the cottage was, as Elizabeth knew, the boundary of the grounds belonging to the big, ruined house. She had looked often at the gate, with its round archway, but she had never passed through it and into the crooked path beyond. The lock was rusty and difficult to turn, she noted, as though Miss Miranda did not often pass that way herself. She felt a flutter of excitement as they went through the gate, feeling that she was about to explore some of those mysteries that had been puzzling more people than herself alone.

The peonies were out indeed, great white drifts of them in a long row below a broken wall. It was not easy to realize that the heaps of blackened stones, covered with vines and lusty wild shrubs, had ever stood for a real dwelling with dining and living rooms and windows opening on the garden. Just facing them, was a stretch of wall still partly unbroken, showing a few windows and a door, charred and blackened by the cruel fire, but still firm on its hinges. A very old cherry tree with a twisted black trunk spread its branches just above. It gave Betsey a creepy feeling to look at that closed entrance and think what ruin and desolation lay behind it.

What had been the lawn was still green and smooth, bordered by a great half circle of pine trees. In the very center of the level stretch of turf was a broad round pool of clear water with a rim of cool gray stone just showing in the thick grass. There was a breeze as Miss Miranda had promised, a gentle wind that moved the heavy branches of the pines and touched the surface of the water. Elizabeth knelt in the grass to peer into the basin, to watch a few lazy fish swimming here and there and to see the mirrored green of the tree-tops all about the edge, with a circle of blue sky reflected in the center.

"You should see it a little later, after dark," said Miss Miranda, leaning over her shoulder to look in also. "That opening between the two biggest trees gives space to reflect the sunset and show the evening star. My father taught me all the stars by showing them to me in the pool; even now I think of June as the time when the Northern Crown shines there in the middle of the basin and of August as when the Swan spreads her wings from one edge to the other."

Perhaps Miss Miranda realized suddenly that she had said more than she intended, for never before had she dropped a hint that this great ruined place had once been her home.

"Look at old Dick," she observed as though to forestall any questioning; "I thought that he would be coming after us."

The solemn figure of the crow came hopping along the path, pausing to peer under stones or behind bushes for snails. With great dignity he stepped across the grass to sit on the rim of the pool.

"Is it deep?" Elizabeth asked, looking down into the quiet water that reflected Dick's image so clearly.

"It is at one side, but not at the other," Miss Miranda answered. "Just here you can touch the bottom if you stretch your arm, but it slopes sharply and is deep enough for swimming over at the other edge. Watch the water and, as it grows darker, you will see the stars come out. Just above the reflection of that tallest pine tree will be the big stars of the Lion, and the curve of the Sickle."

The twilight fell as they sat there talking until, it seemed to Betsey almost by magic, there was the bright star twinkling in the water just as Miss Miranda had said, with other pinpoints of light that grew gradually clearer to show the golden Sickle and the white blur of the Milky Way.

"It is strange how I always loved to watch them," Miss Miranda said, peering into the quiet water as intently as Betsey; "I used to see all the Signs of the Zodiac, that I believed from their name were so mysterious, but that were pictured here so plainly, month by month, that they became as simple as every day. Michael believes that good or ill fortune all goes by luck or charms; some people think that it depends only on what star is the ascendant. He always maintained, after the house was burned, that it was because, when we set out on the journey that left it all alone, we none of us touched both sides of the gatepost as we went through the last time. And it was at the time when the group of stars called the Crab, the most unlucky constellation of them all, was shining in the pool. But I know it was only a bolt of lightning and a wooden roof and nobody at hand to save the place. It was burned to the ground almost before the neighbors saw the smoke and flames among the trees."

"But don't you want to rebuild it? Don't you love it? Don't you want to live here again?" Betsey asked eagerly.

Miss Miranda did not answer. It was evident that Elizabeth had put questions that she had no right to ask, so she pursued the matter no farther. The rising breeze had begun to stir the water once more, so that the stars rocked and twinkled and turned into long streaks of glimmering light. Dick had fluttered across the grass, mounted the broken house wall and now sat there in the dusk, cawing loudly.

"He must see something there behind the wall," observed Elizabeth. "Oh, what is that?"

For Dick, bent on some marauding errand, had swooped down out of their sight, with a harsh cry that was answered immediately by the voice of some unseen person within the house. The blackened door burst open and there came through, first Dick, flying pell mell, then a dark figure outlined for a moment in the doorway. The brighter western sky showed beyond the roofless house, throwing the bent head and broad shoulders into sharp relief. The breeze, driving through the open door, swept forth a flutter of papers, the loose pages of a battered book, that spread far and wide across the grass.

"I beg your pardon," said a voice, "I didn't know any one was here, I thought it was only that mischievous Dick."

The speaker came forward. It was David Warren.

"I come up here to read in the evenings sometimes," he explained in some embarrassment. "It is so quiet and cool, and the sunset light lasts late here on the hill. There is a bit of ceiling left at the corner inside the wall that makes a dry place to keep some books. But I hadn't meant to be trespassing. I had laid my pocketknife on a stone and Dick's eye caught it at once."

He began to gather up the scattered papers which were drifting more and more wildly across the lawn. Betsey ran to give assistance while Miss Miranda assured him that he was not trespassing and was welcome to what hospitality the desolate house afforded. As for Dick he perched on a branch overhead, rocking back and forth apparently with mirth over the mischief he had wrought. He swelled his feathers and gave voice to his one great accomplishment.

"Good morning," he said in his rasping, squeaking voice, "good morning, good morning!"

It was the only thing he had learned to say, and he never made the effort except at moments when he was completely satisfied with himself and all the world.

They sat, all three, beside the pool for a little until the water was sprinkled thick with dancing lights. David was asking many eager questions in regard to Mr. Reynolds' machine. Had there been any more accidents? Were the new experiments turning out well? Did Mr. Reynolds feel encouraged? There were many other queries besides, about gas turbines and lubricating systems, too technical for even Miss Miranda to be able to answer. They both walked home with Elizabeth through the warm dark and left her at her door. She had not much to say, for something was puzzling her greatly. In gathering up the scattered papers she had found one among the rest that looked strangely and disagreeably familiar. The light was dim but she could not mistake the drawing, that intricate and much-hated figure, the frustum of a pyramid. She could not conceive why David Warren should be troubling his head with such matters. Indeed, there seemed to be a good many things that she could not understand at all.

CHAPTER V

AS THE CROW FLIES

Michael was trimming the grape vines, ably assisted by Dick, who sidled along the trellis, keeping up a fluent stream of inarticulate advice and trying, apparently, to get his horny toes or his long black bill cut off by the snapping shears.

"Oh, get along with you," cried Michael at last, stung to impatience by having cut off the wrong twig in his effort to avoid injuring the inquisitive bird. "Go on about your business and leave me be."

He gave his black companion a friendly cuff that pushed him off the trellis and launched him into flight. Dick swooped across the garden, where Betsey stood laughing at him and at Michael's irritation, and flew to the top of the stone wall where he sat scolding with all his might.

"He is not wise to do that," commented Miss Miranda. "When he caws so loudly he is apt to bring the wild crows and they do not like him."

Friendly as Dick was with all members of the human race, he was plainly not on good terms with his own kind. Luxurious living had made him larger and sleeker than they, but a less agile flier. He led a lazy life and was not so practiced or swift on the wing as those hard, wiry birds who gained their living by gleaning in the fields. Even as Betsey watched, a rusty, wild crow flew up, attracted by his cawing, and perched on the wall beside him, followed by another and another.

"Oh, look," Betsey cried, "they are pecking him. And here come some others!"

The wild crows had fallen on poor Dick with vicious, stabbing bills and were being joined by a rapidly increasing crowd of comrades. The clamor that arose was deafening, Dick's pathetic caws being mixed with the angry, harsh cries of his assailants, all of whom were jealous, it seemed, of his plump sides and shining coat. He took flight finally and sailed away toward the top of the hill, pursued by a trailing cloud of chattering enemies.

"The wild crows have always hated him," Miss Miranda said anxiously, "and he will never learn not to provoke them. There are so many this time that I am afraid they will peck him to death."

Elizabeth set off in pursuit, hoping to find where they had alighted and to drive off the attacking birds, but, although she ran with all speed across the lawn and through the gate in the wall, she lost sight of the flock over the crest of the hill. The continued uproar, however, of angry crow voices guided her onward so that she followed farther and farther, hoping every moment to come close enough to scatter the struggling group with a stone. She found traces of the battle here and there, in scattered black feathers that drifted over the grass. She would not give up the chase so long as poor Dick, driven ever farther from home, still called for help from his human friends with a voice that grew continually weaker.

Past the ruined house she ran, and down the farther slope of the hill, through unexplored country where thick hedges and overgrown flower beds showed the traces of an abandoned formal garden. There was a sundial, so covered with vines that no one, even at high noon, could have read the hour on its mossy face, and a tumbledown arbor smothered in climbing yellow roses. More and more she realized what a beautiful place this must have been where Miss Miranda had once lived, but Dick's unhappy progress gave her little time for observation.

Over the lower wall swept the chase and over the wall went Betsey in pursuit, clambering up one side by the aid of a leaning pear tree and half sliding, half tumbling down on the other. She reached the ground with rather of a thud, but she picked herself up and ran on, paying no attention to the jarring fall. The way went across plowed fields now, and through bramble hedges, past a stream or two and even into a swampy meadow where the green sod sank under Elizabeth's footsteps and left muddy pools that sucked at her shoes. Finally a farmer's cottage at the edge of a river came in sight and, to her relief here, the running fight seemed to have come to an end. She saw the wild crows perching and rocking on the boughs of a big tree before the gate, cawing in such shrill-voiced anger that she was certain they must have been somehow robbed of their prey. As she came panting into the farmyard she observed there was a pigeonhouse high up under the peak of the barn roof and it was plain, from the way in which the astonished white birds were bursting out of doors and windows, that it was in their dwelling that the harassed and desperate Dick had taken refuge.

A surprised farmer, not knowing quite what to make of such a breathless and disheveled stranger, led her up the narrow stairs that climbed to the pigeon loft and opened the door upon the rows of perches and nests. Dick came fluttering to her at once, a weary and bedraggled bird, with his bright plumage torn and his head bleeding and plucked almost bare. She held him carefully as she picked her way down the steep stairs again, unable to help laughing at his croaking attempts to tell just what had happened.

The farmer's wife, a hearty, friendly woman, insisted that Elizabeth sit down in the shade of the big tree and rest a little.

"I will bring you a drink of water; just wait a minute until I draw some fresh from the well," she said.

She went bustling away, leaving Betsey very glad to sit there quietly and regain her breath. It was a pleasant place, with the grassy slope before the house going down to the river, crossed, just here, by a little bridge. She sat watching the smooth water with its swinging lily pads and the quaint stone arch of the old bridge, thinking what a peaceful and picturesque spot it was.

"It looks almost like one of Aunt Susan's picture post cards," she reflected, "only I don't think Aunt Susan would stop long at any such quiet and out-of-the-way place as this."

There had been a gay-colored shower of bright postals from Aunt Susan lately, ships and hotels and panoramas of tropical scenes where the inhabitants seemed to have nothing to do but sit about on banks of flowers with brilliant green palms as a background. There were also bits of scenes like this one, places of historic association, chosen, Betsey knew, not because her aunt had spent much time viewing such spots, but because that type of post-card gave more space for correspondence. Aunt Susan never wrote letters. Each one of her pictured messages, however, ended with the words, "You ought to be with me." But they had ceased to arouse any longings in Betsey's heart.

The farmer's wife presently returned with a glass of milk, some fresh rolls she had just taken from the oven, and honey from the row of blue beehives that stood at the foot of the garden.

"Joe tells me that you said the bird belongs to Miss Miranda Reynolds," she said, seating herself ponderously at the other end of the bench while Elizabeth partook of the welcome refreshment, and scattered crumbs for Dick. "I suppose it must have belonged to Mr. Ted Reynolds before he went away. He was a great boy for pets always. I will never forget how he brought home a young alligator and let it get lost in the house so that the laundress finally found it at the bottom of her washtub of clothes."

"Oh, did you know them?" cried Elizabeth. "Did you know Miss Miranda's brother and her cousin and that big house on the hill?"

"I was housemaid there for seven years before I was married," responded the woman. "It was Miss Miranda herself arranged the flowers for my wedding and gave me my wedding clothes. A dear beautiful place it was, that house. I would never have come away from it except to marry Joe."

She smoothed her white apron over her knees and went on in eager reminiscence.

"I can remember every inch of it and am always telling the children about what I saw there. One thing I can't forget was a big desk with glass doors and such strange ornaments on the shelves. There was a little pine tree carved out of something that looked like green glass. I used to stop and stare at it every time I dusted. Did they save that, do you know, when the place was burned?"

"Yes," Betsey replied to the other's evident relief, "the toy-cupboard is safe at the cottage."

"I have always been waiting to hear that they were going to rebuild the house," the woman went on, "but year after year goes by and they keep on living in the little cottage. Miss Miranda loved her home so, I know she is sick at heart to go back to it. I don't understand it."

"Nor do I," observed Betsey with a sigh.

"It may be because of that work her father is doing," suggested the other shrewdly. "Such things do take a power of money and I am certain Miss Miranda would do without anything rather than have him give it up. She would think that was her share of the success that she has always felt certain was coming. He has worked at the thing ten years now, he should be finishing it one of these days." She dropped her voice to question Betsey with the earnestness of real friendship and devotion. "I don't see her very often now, but I think of her all the time. Do you—do you think she is happy?"

Betsey shook her head slowly.

"I am afraid not," she replied.

"Her father was always so anxious that she should be, he was absorbed in his work but he never would forget about that. He depended on her and consulted with her even when she was not a great deal bigger than you, yet was running the whole place and keeping the two boys in order. Mr. Ted adored her and she him, he was a fine fellow. But that Cousin

Donald, we in the kitchen could never abide him with his sharp selfish face and his overbearing ways. She could face him down, but at heart she was afraid of him, I used to think. He could say such cruel, cutting things to hurt her, although she would never show it. I have known Mr. Ted to black his eye for him, for all he was so much younger, when he thought his sister had been made unhappy. Proud they are, and sensitive to the quick, father and daughter and son. That Donald Reynolds was an alien amongst them."

Her flood of recollection went on, but began to wander to such details as Joe's courting and how they were married, in which Betsey did not feel quite so great an interest, so that at last she took advantage of a slight pause in the talk to say that she must go. There was one more question she wished to ask.

"That cousin, what did he look like?"

"Oh, insignificant like," was the somewhat vague answer. "He had black hair and eyes that were greenish, a little, they always put me in mind of boiled gooseberries. He was the sort of person bound to prosper, and after Miss Miranda helped to bring him up I wonder how he can see her want for anything. There now, if you must go I have a setting of eggs I've wanted to send over to her for her poultry yard, they're the best in the state."

She brought Betsey the package, rather apologetic that it should prove larger than she had intended.

"I just tucked some duck eggs into the box, too. This is an uncommon breed that Joe got me, and splendid for market. I'm sorry it's such a big bundle and the way home so long. I do wish the horses weren't all in the field or Joe could take you home in the cart. You tell Miss Reynolds that those are with Clara Bassett's love and that she will never forget her. I will be over to see her myself, first chance I get."

Her kind hostess stood watching her from the gate as Elizabeth set off homeward. She had been directed to take the path along the river bank and then turn into a cart track that went over the hill and she had been warned that it was "quite a ways." She discovered herself to be more tired after her long chase than she had thought, and beginning to feel a few aches due to her jarring tumble over the wall. She tramped steadily onward, nevertheless, Dick riding on her shoulder and the bundle of eggs tucked under her arm. It was of awkward shape and size, and would slip no matter how she held it.

The path along the river did not seem to be taking her in the direction of home and it was discouragingly rough and stony. She sat down to rest, with her feet dangling over the bank above the water and began to think over what she had been hearing.

"Everybody who knows Miss Miranda seems to want to make her happy," she reflected, "and the strange thing is that nobody can!"

She sat for some time listening to the cool splashing water slip away below her feet, then with a sigh got up to go onward.

"I think I'd better take a short cut across the fields," she decided. "It won't be half so far and I'm sure I can find the way. If only I don't drop the eggs."

The flight of a crow is supposed to be a direct route, but not the way of a crow pursued by a flock of his jealous kin. The chase that Dick had led her had been so crooked and confused that it was difficult indeed to find which was the shortest way home. She pushed through hedges, hurried down by-paths, stumbled into tangles of wild blackberry vines, but was not at all sure that she was making any real progress.

The round wooded hills and squares of well-kept field and meadow all looked much alike to her. A big house among the trees, showing tall stacks of brick chimneys and a tiled roof was, moreover, so completely unfamiliar that she became still more perplexed. The afternoon was coming to an end, she grew wearier and wearier and the box in her arms seemed continually heavier and more awkward. At last she stood still, having completely lost her bearings.

"Oh, Dick," she said forlornly, "can't you show me the way home?"

Dick, however, quite unabashed by the trouble he had caused, flew from her shoulder and began gravely hopping about the grass at the side of the way. Betsey looked about her desperately and saw a half-plowed field at some distance, bordered by a hedge.

"There may be some one at work there," she thought, "and I can ask the way."

But it seemed far indeed to drag her heavy feet up the hill, through a spur of woodland and along a rough lane between two hedges. She could hear the soft trampling of a horse's hoofs on the loose earth and a cheerful whistling that told her that some sort of help must be at hand. Scrambling up the bank, she found a gap in the bushes, thrust her head through and began—

"If you please, will you tell me—oh!"

For the horse standing in the furrow, just unharnessed from the plow, was the big white Dobbin and the plowman was David Warren.

He came pushing through the hedge at once and, before a word was said, took the heavy parcel from her.

"You and Dick seem to be rather far from home," he observed cheerfully.

"Be careful, it's eggs!" she warned as he thrust the bundle under his arm.

"Dobbin and I were just going home," he said. "Wait until I can drive him around by the gate and he'll be proud to carry you. He's not much of a saddle horse. His back is more like a seat in a Pullman car."

He was quite right, for weary Betsey, once perched on the wide back, thought it the most luxurious spot on earth. The gentle old horse seemed entirely willing and, even when Dick came fluttering up to perch on one of the brass knobs of the heavy harness, he merely looked around with an expression of mild wonder to see what new sort of rider this might be. While they moved slowly up the lane, Elizabeth gave an account of the crow's misadventures.

"Dick, you old rascal, if you ever give so much trouble again I will wring your neck," the boy said severely, whereat the black bird cocked his eye and seemed to chuckle silently over the manifest untruth of such a threat.

There followed a little pause in their talk as they moved onward up the slope with Dobbin's great feet rustling in the high weeds and his long shadow slipping so quietly ahead of them across the grass. The dropping sunlight was falling on David's uncovered head and turning it from red-brown to coppery gold. They reached the crest of the slope where an opening in the trees afforded a wide view of that same stretch of valley across which Betsey had sat gazing that day she was caught by the shower before her first visit to Miss Miranda. Here, without a word of bidding the big horse came to a stop. David laughed, and laid an affectionate hand on his neck.

"Dobbin always knows where I like to stand and look over the valley," he said. "We stop here so often that now he never goes by. I like to look at those college towers and wonder how I can go there some day."

"Oh, are you going there?" cried Betsey with an excited wriggle that nearly unseated her; "so am I—if nothing happens."

She thought of the geometrical and historical difficulties in the way and sighed.

"A great deal will have to happen before I get there," David remarked light-heartedly, "but I mean to manage it somehow. Perhaps only Dobbin knows how much I think about it while I work here in my uncle's fields."

"Is that your uncle's house?" questioned Betsey, looking up at the big chimneys above the trees.

"Yes, and all this land is his, up to Somerset Lane. He is away a great deal and expects me rather to keep an eye on things, but of course I work on the farm too. There is really almost no one else to do it with all the labor crowding into the cities. I try to study by myself at night but—I don't get very far. There are some places where I think I will stick forever."

"Oh," exclaimed Betsey, suddenly seeing the explanation of that puzzling page that had fallen into her hands the night David's papers blew away, "do you find it hard to prove what is the volume of the frustum of a pyramid?"

"Do I?" returned David from the bottom of his heart. His freckled face crinkled into a delighted grin as he looked up at her. "Don't tell me that there is some one else who finds it as mysterious as I do! 'The frustum of a pyramid is equal to three other pyramids,' I can get that far and I can even understand the first one, but the second is almost too much for me, and the third is quite impossible."

"And I," returned Betsey gravely, "if I can once get the first one, I can go on to the end. It is just at the beginning that I always come to grief."

"Perhaps you could help me and I could help you," David suggested excitedly. "I would sleep easier at night if I could once get those three pyramids into my head. I have my book in that corner up at the ruined house. I believe we have time to look it up before you must go home. Come up, Dobbin!"

The willing old horse strode forward again.

"It's not just geometry that bothers me," Elizabeth confessed. "We had some questions in history to-day and it frightened me to have them show how little I knew. We were asked who were the Barbary pirates and what was the greatest time of America's merchant marine. Those are just the things I never can remember."

"History doesn't seem so hard," returned David, "except that, if you study it without a teacher, you get so interested in some parts that you forget to pay any attention to the others. You say that they asked you about the merchant marine and America's ships? Now I never thought of paying any attention to that. Hurry, Dobbin. I begin to think that we have no time to lose."

They turned into Somerset Lane, hastened up the final slope and left the white horse tied to the cottage gate. Miss Miranda seemed to be still at work in the garden, so they deposited Dick and the package of eggs in the kitchen and went scurrying across the lawn to the gate in the wall. If they were to vanquish their common enemy before dark it was necessary to make some speed.

The key of the gate stood in the lock, but was stiff and rusty and creaked as David forced its turning. They hurried along the grassy path, stooping under the low-hanging branches and brushing aside the unpruned shrubs. For some reason they trod more quietly and spoke more softly when they came within the circle of the open lawn. It seemed very breathless and silent in the late afternoon sunlight, this beautiful place with its black, motionless pine trees, its gleaming pool and its empty, ruined house open to the sky.

"I wish I understood about all this," said Betsey, almost under her breath as they stood a moment by the still pool, "why the house was never rebuilt, why Miss Miranda works so hard and looks so worried and so sad."

"There's something strange about the place," David agreed, "and Miss Miranda and her father are not like other people. Sometimes she seems to me like a person who sees a great trouble coming nearer and nearer and doesn't know what to do."

"I wish," Betsey said with a deep wistful sigh, "oh, how I wish we could help her!"

"Perhaps we can," returned David. He was looking about him intently, as though already deciding what could be done.

"I think," Betsey went on, "that nothing could please me more in the world than to see Miss Miranda lose that worried, frightened look, and to know that she is comfortable and happy again."

David shook his head.

"I want more than that," he declared. "I'm not going to be satisfied until everything is as it was, until this house is rebuilt and they are living here again, safe and peaceful and at home. If we are to help at all, we should work for that. Shall we try?"

The ambition seemed to be rather an overwhelming one. To Elizabeth, as she looked about the still garden, sleeping in the level sunshine, it appeared that only something miraculous could awake it into stirring life again. But how much happiness it would bring! She often wondered what that strained look in Miss Miranda's eyes could mean; she understood now, it was the look of some one who wants to go home.

"Yes," she answered bravely, "we will try."

It was a great undertaking and they shook hands upon it. They did not look very large, those two, under the shadow of the tall pines and of the vast, broken walls, as they stood beside the pool. They seemed, indeed, to be pledging themselves to the following of an impossible purpose. Yet, as Betsey's firm vigorous hand met David's hard brown one, suddenly it became a plan that might come true.

CHAPTER VI

THE BARBARY PIRATES

Although there was not much more than an hour of daylight left, the two friends put off their mathematical researches and spent a little time in exploring the ruins of the house. David opened the heavy, charred door of his own refuge and showed Betsey the remains of the room inside with the fragments of a brick staircase that had once wound upward above it.

"This end of the house was not destroyed at once, I think," he said, "and I believe a good deal of the furniture was got out of it, things that you can still see at the cottage. The roof fell after a day or two and carried the walls with it, so that there are some relics left in the ruins still. This little room under the stairs must have been a den belonging to Miss Miranda's brother Ted, for I found a pair of spurs and a rusty rifle, a melted silver cup, and some such things here. Beyond must have been the library and a conservatory behind, at least there are mountains of broken glass beside that wall."

From here, then, had been rescued the toy-cupboard and such pieces of heavy mahogany furniture as were still in use in the cottage and which stood out in such strong contrast to the very plain chairs and tables of painted pine that filled the rest of the Reynolds' abode. The ivy that had once climbed the high walls, that had crept around the leaded windows and festooned the pillared doorway, now spread its mats of green and its slim, rose colored tendrils over the desolate ruins and covered what it could. Broken pictures still showed half buried under bricks and plaster, while a mirror leaned crookedly against a wall, showing fantastic patterns of shivered glass.

"This must have been the kitchen," David went on as they progressed farther. "Be careful how you climb about, these old walls are none too solid."

He himself, however, went clambering up heedless of precaution, his only thought being, apparently, that harm might come to Betsey.

"That place beyond I've never explored," he said; "wait here a minute until I get to the top of that ridge of bricks. The weight of both of us might make it begin to slide."

"Don't," she objected, "it doesn't look safe at all. Can't you go to the other—"

He had left her protests unheeded and had clambered half way up the slope of broken débris, when she saw it begin to tremble under his feet, then suddenly give way and carry him down out of her sight. She ran to the edge to see, squeezed through the cleft made by the collapse of the brick-heap and slid down after, to find David, a trifle scratched and with his red hair full of brick-dust, standing gazing about him with untroubled interest.

"This must have been the end of the house where the fire started," he commented. "See how much blacker the walls are and how even the bricks are burned. And look, that must be a part of one of the chimneys still left standing: you can see that the lightning struck it and split it to the very base. I wonder, with all the frost and rain since the fire, that it hasn't fallen long ago. I don't quite understand what this room is. It seems to have been away from the house and on a lower level."

Elizabeth balanced on the edge of a stone and looked at the confusion about her, where rusty heaps of metal and coils of wire lay amid the other rubbish.

"It must have been Mr. Reynolds' workshop," she suggested, "and see, even those steel bars are melted together. The fire must surely have been hottest just here."

"I believe you're right." David was picking his way about looking at the broken engine parts and the melted bits of steel. "I suppose he was working even then on that same invention. I think it ought to be a very great thing when it is done."

"I think," began Betsey, "that—oh, look, look!"

She stood transfixed with dismay, staring at something behind him. David gave one glance and knew better than to pause and look again.

"Quick," he cried, and, seizing her hand, dragged her, almost headlong, across the open space and up another slope of sliding bricks.

The old chimney, split by the lightning and weakened by fire and frost, was ready to tumble at the slightest shock and had received its final impetus from the collapse of the neighboring wall. As Betsey looked at it the whole mass was tottering and, but for David's quickness, would have engulfed them both. As it was they were nearly smothered by the cloud of dust and crumbled mortar. Blinded and breathless, they scrambled out of the hollow to safety. David's dusty face had not lost its cheerful smile, but he spoke with great decision.

"I was very wrong to let you go in there," he said. "I might have seen that the whole place is shaky and that the walls have been collapsing, little by little, for years. We will not go near this end of it at least, again."

Elizabeth knelt by the pool to wash the dust from her face and hands, while David, having done the same, went to fetch his geometry book.

"Now," he said, sitting down by her with something of a sigh, "we really must, I suppose, begin on that tiresome pyramid."

They had a gay session there under the trees before the light began to fail, while each, by instructing the other, succeeded in mastering all former difficulties. In the end they fell to firing rapid questions at each other, Betsey trying to trip David in his fluent statement of the theorem, he in turn lying in wait for her on obscure points of the proof, until neither could be shaken from the thoroughness with which knowledge was now entrenched.

"How lucky it is," said Betsey, putting down the book and leaning back with her elbow on the rim of the pool, "that each of us stuck in a different place! I hope it will often be that way and that we can help each other more. Now why—" her method of finding things out was apt to be by blunt questioning, a habit she could not easily put aside, "why are you getting ready for college all alone when it is so much easier to do it by going to school?"

David stretched his long legs in the grass and looked fixedly down into the water.

"I was nearly ready to go two years ago," he explained, "but I left school instead and began to work, since I was too young to go to war. I have no father and things were not going very well with my mother and me while the war lasted, and besides every pair of hands was needed for the extra labor. Now that peace has come, our affairs are better again and I could go to college next autumn, except that there are some things I still have to learn. I took this place with my uncle because I knew the work would only last through the summer and then would leave me free. I have a cousin who is a professor over at the college and who helps me with my work, but I don't have time to go to him often."

Elizabeth was thinking, as she sat looking into the water, of how she would feel if further education became suddenly as complicated for her as it was for him. The knowledge of his difficulties tended to arouse her own flagging zeal, so that she began to feel that obstinate pyramids and elusive pirates could not really stand in the way of true determination. As she sat reflecting, footsteps approached along the grassy path and Miss Miranda's voice sounded behind them.

"I have been looking for you everywhere," she said. "Dick has been trying to tell me about his adventures, but has only succeeded in convincing me that it was a very desperate affair. Poor battered bird, he will not sit on the wall and call out challenges to other crows soon again. I have invited myself to have supper with you here beside the pool, while you tell me all that has happened."

She set down the basket that she had been carrying and began to spread a table cloth on the grass.

"Michael is feeding Dobbin," she said, "and I have telephoned to Betsey's house, so that all that you have to do is to sit down and eat."

The suggestion was adopted with alacrity, for the appetites of the two were keen, and their own evening meals seemed far away. Amid much mirth was told the tale of poor Dick's misfortunes, of his headlong flight from his enemies and of the amazement of the pigeons on whose hospitality he had so unceremoniously thrust himself. Of her talk with the farmer's wife, Betsey did not say so much, only delivered her messages and accounted for the eggs.

"I thought I would drop them a hundred times," she said at the end. "I never knew that eggs could grow so heavy."

She sat lazily on the grass, feeling rested and content, unmindful for any further exertion than to dabble her fingers in the quiet pool. A shimmering band of sunset light dyed the opposite half of the basin as though the water had been set on fire. Miss Miranda, leaning comfortably against a tree, had taken out her knitting.

"There is something wrong with Michael to-night," she observed as she clicked the needles in and out. "He is sitting on the bench by the gate staring straight before him and not even smoking his pipe. When I asked him what was the matter he only growled out that a black cat ran across his path last night and that trouble was bound to follow. I suppose he is reciting spells to himself, to drive off the evil. Certainly there was no use in talking to him."

Elizabeth was looking up at the ruined house, trying to imagine how it had seemed, with lights in the windows, with fires on its deserted hearthstones, with all the warm brightness of home shining through its open doorway. Miss Miranda must have been thinking, with far greater and more painful clearness, of much the same thing.

"I used to believe," she said suddenly in midst of a silence, "when I came home from school and crossed the lawn to that side door, that burned, marred door in the wall that is the only one left, that it opened on the dearest place in the world. The big, black cherry tree that grows beside it used to spread such a cloud of white blossoms every spring! I always thought, when I heard people talk of the narrow gate of Heaven, that it must look just like my little dark door under the blooming cherry tree."

She moved over to sit by Elizabeth at the edge of the pool.

"It is not easy to come home to an empty, silent house that is not really home," she went on. "No one knows that better than I, my dear, or would like more to make it up to you."

Betsey moved closer and smiled up at her gratefully.

"You do make it up to me," she said.

David, who was lying stretched out at Miss Miranda's feet was busy at a task of his own. It seemed that he was a persistent boy who would never lay aside a piece of work until every detail that he could think of had been added to make it complete. He had fetched some clay from the far end of the garden and was modeling the frustum of a pyramid and those three confusing portions into which it could be divided. Betsey watched him idly, quite content that he should have the labor and she the benefit. He demonstrated them with a flourish on the smooth rim of the pool.

"You make it so clear," remarked Miranda, "that I almost understand it myself, although I had forgotten it ten years ago."

"Your father must know all about such things," David said rather wistfully; "it discourages me to think of how much he knows. Do you suppose he would care to have—to have any one help him in his shop, just to sharpen tools and screw bolts and run errands?"

"He needs some one like that very greatly," Miss Miranda answered. "As a rule he likes to do his work alone for fear the news of what he is trying to make will get about before he is ready. But I know you well enough to be certain that you will give away no secrets."

Elizabeth drew her dripping hand from the water and took up one of the pyramids.

"I never thought I could understand it so clearly," she said, "and now if I could only remember about the Barbary pirates and the merchant marine, I really could be almost sure of going to college."

"Barbary pirates?" repeated Miss Miranda. "I happen to know something of them, myself. How do they come to trouble you when they have all been dead so long?"

"Oh, I just don't seem to be able to remember when they lived, or what they did," Betsey sighed. "They seem to come in that dull middle period in the history, between the Revolution and the Civil War, when nothing particular ever seemed to happen and most of the Presidents were men whose names you never heard before. It's all very difficult."

"Do you remember," returned Miss Miranda, "that little green tree that you saw in my toy cupboard, the first day that you came? It was put there by my great-grandfather, who fought against those self-same pirates and helped to put an end to their wrongdoing. If I should tell you how he came into possession of the tree, I believe you could remember better what happened in those early days and how America built up her shipping, that merchant marine about which I have heard you groan. Would you like to hear?"

"We would," answered the two in a single breath.

"And may I go and bring the tree to show David?" Elizabeth asked. She scarcely waited for permission but was off down the path having quite forgotten her former weariness.

Michael was sitting on the bench as Miss Miranda had said, and would not even respond to her greeting as she passed. He had been so friendly of recent days that she stopped, surprised, and turned back to question him.

"What is the matter Michael? Is it really the black cat that troubles you so?"

"Matter enough," he returned morosely, "even without the black cat. There has been trouble brewing for long and I am thinking it is about to break."

"But why? What trouble? What makes you think so?" Betsey pressed her questions anxiously. But his answers were most unsatisfactory.

"Oh, just trouble. And how do I know it is coming soon? I feel it in my bones like."

He would say no more and she was forced to go about her errand. As she crossed the lawn by the house she saw that the workshop door was open to the warm night air and that Mr. Reynolds was as busy as ever inside. It made a quaint picture, the shadowy room, the brilliant circle of light, the old man's intent, intelligent face bent over his work, the black crow sitting immovable as a statue on the corner of the table. A pleasant noise of quietly whirring wheels came out of the door, a peaceful, comfortable song that mingled with the cheery chirp of a cricket in the grass. It was such a happy, untroubled scene. No presentiment of evil could be lurking that night in any bones, but Michael's.

When Elizabeth returned with the little tree, David was as entranced with it as she had been. It stood on the edge of the basin in the last of the failing twilight and, in its airy grace of form and glittering of jade and jewels, it seemed scarcely a thing of reality at all. Miss Miranda laid her knitting on her knee for the light was gone at last. The sunset colors had faded in the water and the fireflies were beginning to wink and shine in the shadows of the pine trunks as she began.

CHAPTER VII

THE TREE OF JADE

From the time when they first went to the dame school to learn their letters, Jonathan Adams and Humphrey Reynolds spent most of their waking hours in each other's company. They looked for birds' nests together in the woods at the edge of the broad Susquehanna River, they paddled along its marshy banks, they played absorbing games in that busy, entrancing place, Jonathan's father's shipyard. Or they would stand side by side watching a great ship of war come sailing up the bay, a flying vision of square white sails and darkly outlined rigging, the vessel that was commanded by Captain Reynolds, Humphrey's father. The two boys talked much of what they would do when they were men; they would sit for long hours on the wharf, their legs dangling above the water, discussing the future.

"I am going into the Navy like my father," Humphrey would say, "and I intend to sail in the finest and fastest ship of the whole fleet to the very ends of the world and back again. And I will have you for executive officer, Jonathan."

"No," Jonathan would return seriously, "I get sick when I go to sea and I don't like hardtack and salt pork. No, I will stop at home in my father's yards and some day I will build a ship that is a real ship and not just tubs like these."

They parted when they were seventeen and did not meet again for years, for Humphrey went into the Navy as he had planned and Jonathan, with mallet and chisel in hand and with that sober, earnest air that always clung to him, was already at work in his father's shipyard. In time he became master of the entire business, while Humphrey was scouring the seas, sailing on just those far voyages of which he had so often dreamed. Jonathan had his dreams also, but he did not speak of them, only toiled away at building the heavy, sturdy vessels that carried America's trade overseas early in the last century. Honest ships they were and reliable, as sure of coming to port as though they had belonged to the age of steam, but oh, how long it took them to make a voyage! In the privacy of his dingy little office Jonathan, with the door fastened, would push aside the clutter of plans and drawings and would get out the model of a strange vessel, sharp, slender and graceful, with a hull like a racing yacht. He would set it upon the bench to carve a little here, to alter a curve by a hair's breadth there, or merely to stand staring at it sometimes for hours at a time, staring and thinking.

One day when he was so standing, utterly lost in some unspoken vision, there came a knock at the door, followed by an impatient second one and a thunderous third, all during the moment of time that it took the shipmaster to put out of sight his beloved model. When the door was opened there strode in a tall sunburned person in blue uniform, Humphrey Reynolds come at last to see his old comrade, bringing a roll of government documents under his arm.

"Congress has taken a sudden turn toward increasing the Navy," the young officer explained, "and the orders are going out to build twelve ships in haste. One of the contracts is to come to you, if you will take it. They are even in such need that they have not laid down the specifications to the last bolt and rope's end, so that the man who builds this ship and the officer who superintends the construction, can really have something to say about the design."

He looked his old friend very steadily in the eye and saw a slow smile of deep, unspoken delight dawn upon the shipbuilder's face. Jonathan Adams' hard hands did not often tremble, but they shook a little now as he reached up to the shelf above the bench and brought down his model.

"I have been thinking about such a design since I was ten years old," he said, "and the chance to build it has come at last. We will make them a real ship, Humphrey, and the whole world will open its eyes when it sees you sail her."

She grew up quickly on the ways, that ship of their very hearts' desire, with her bowsprit standing far out over the neighboring street, and with people stopping in the lane to watch Jonathan's whole force of workmen toiling up and down her timbered sides. Old Navy officers who had seen, some of them, the ships of the Revolution, and who had all fought in the War of Eighteen-twelve, would come to inspect her and would shake their heads.

"Look at that high, sharp bow," one would say; "such a craft will never be seaworthy in the world. Why can't these young fellows stick to the models we have tried out for them?"

"And see the spread of sail this drawing shows," another would comment, pointing fiercely with a stubby forefinger; "why, the whole ridiculous affair will capsize in the first good puff of wind! I'm thankful I don't have to go to sea in her."

But the two comrades closed their ears and sat, often far into the night, in the cramped little office, poring over drawings and comparing designs.

"You have her thought out to the last ring, block and halyard," Humphrey would say, "and you never even knew if you could build her. What a dreamer you are!"

"It takes dreaming to keep a man at his work," Jonathan would answer. "How do you think I would have had the patience, all these years, to drive wooden pins into cross-timbers, or to mend the rigging of limping coastwise schooners if I had not been thinking of just such a ship as this, and seen her, in my mind's eye, putting to sea under full sail, to smash every sailing record that has been known?"

The day of the launching came, then the stepping of the giant masts, the completing of the rigging and the bending of the new sails.

"The *West Wind* will be ready for sea in two weeks now," Humphrey said, one morning at breakfast to Miranda Reynolds—she was my great-grandmother and I was named for her. They had been married only a month and this would be his first cruise since their wedding. She drew her breath quickly, she had not known it was to be so soon.

"People say," she began hesitatingly, "old sailors and longshoremen and even the Naval officers that have been here, say that the *West Wind* will never stand a storm."

"They are the kind of men," Humphrey scoffed, "who would be sailing vessels of the model of the Ark, did not people like Jonathan Adams have the courage, sometimes, to build something new. No, the *West Wind* is going to teach all the shipmasters something they never knew before, when once she sets sail. And we expect to clear for Gibraltar in less than a month. Why, Miranda, you're not crying?"

"No," declared Miranda, choking bravely, for tears have no place in a sea captain's household. She even managed to muster a watery smile. "I wonder what you will leave behind you in foreign parts this time, your gold snuffbox, perhaps."

It was a longstanding joke that young Captain Reynolds was so careless of his possessions that he never came home from a voyage without having lost or mislaid by the way everything he had. But the gold snuffbox had survived several cruises, since it was the most valuable thing he owned. It had been presented to him by the citizens of his town when he had come home from sea some years ago, after, so he expressed, "a miserable Algerine pirate lay alongside him and insisted on being taken."

It is probably only a short paragraph in your history book and possibly a very dull one that tells you how, a little more than a hundred years ago, the seas swarmed with pirates whose home ports were the North African cities of Algiers, Tripoli and Tunis. The great nations of Europe and, with them, the young United States, used to buy safety from these lawless Barbary States by sending them gifts and tribute. But when, finally, the Pasha of Tripoli sent word to our President that his last gift was not large enough and that more must be sent, the answer was a fleet of American warships and the bombardment of the astonished monarch's seaports. There were many spirited encounters during that little war, many feats of daring seamanship of which history has lost sight among the greater events that have followed. But for years after the struggle was over, the United States Navy still policed that foreign sea with such thoroughness that the pirate craft that dared venture from port were bold and desperate indeed.

It was thither that the *West Wind* was to sail, with dispatches for the Commodore of the Mediterranean Fleet. At last the ship was ready, a rare and beautiful sight with her slim hull, her rows of guns and her towering reach of silvery new canvas.

She sailed with the early tide, at daybreak of a mid-April morning, a ghostly fairy-like thing, slipping away in the gray light and the mist of dawn. Miranda stood on the dock to watch her go, with Jonathan beside her staring fixedly after his winged dream, flying at last beyond the seas.

"There will be tales to tell when she comes back," he said at last, "and I look for her to cut down the sailing time by three, four, five days, perhaps. She has borne away the hearts of both of us but she is a good ship and she will bring them back again."

His stout faith in his ship was matched only by Humphrey's unwavering confidence. Others might have said that this maiden voyage of his first command was a heart-breaking one, for many of his men were untrained seamen, grumbling at their narrow quarters and heavy labor, while the art of handling the new vessel was, in itself, not easy to acquire. The weather was boisterous and the winds fitful, but the *West Wind* did not betray the two good friends who had brought her into being. The storms lent her wings so that, at last, anxiety and discontent gave way entirely to pride in the speed that she was making. There was a certain grizzled old sailor, however, who openly discredited all claims of the ship's prowess, and who even refused to believe the evidence of the day's reckoning.

"Twenty-three days is the best she will do," he vowed over and over again. "I will stake a year's pay on it that she can't make an hour less."

Yet, on the nineteenth day of their passage, a warm, gusty afternoon of early May, when the far horizon swam in haze, it was he who came himself to the captain and broke through all etiquette to report, round-eyed with amazement—

"There's land been sighted, sir, and I don't understand it at all. It—it looks like Gibraltar!"

So she came through the gates of the Mediterranean, a gentle breeze behind her, "sails all filled and asleep" as the seamen said, a swift slender hull under a cloud of snowy canvas. She pushed into the straits where had plied back and forth the daring Phœnician craft, the Roman galleys and the high-pooped ships of Venice and of Spain, but she was no lesser vessel than any one of them, for she was the first of the Yankee clipper ships!

I have never seen those North African cities, Tangier and Tunis and the rest, and I have no doubt that to-day they are very little like what Humphrey Reynolds saw. But his stories have come down to me so clear and vivid, that I almost feel that I have known those very places with their white houses, their tropical green, the confusion and chatter of foreign tongues in the narrow streets, the hushed silence of the wide, walled gardens. For long months the American warships would lie off these ports, keeping a watchful eye upon the doings of the dusky potentates and arch-pirates who ruled them. The officers and men would go ashore to stare at the strange sights and to bargain for souvenirs among the street vendors, seemingly oblivious of the scowling, hostile faces about them.

It was in Tripoli on a day when Captain Reynolds was walking from one dark cupboard of a shop to another, looking for some fitting gift to take home to Miranda, that he was suddenly startled by the sight of a pale face among all those dusky ones. It was not white, but yellow, and belonged to an old Chinaman, as dried up and withered as a mummy, who had somehow wandered, a rare thing in those days, to this African city and kept a little shop there among the Moors, Arabs and Berbers of Tripoli. His wares were different from the others and very new indeed to Humphrey's eyes, for just such carvings and silks did not often find their way to America. The old man invited the officer to come inside where more articles stood upon the narrow shelves and where Humphrey had almost decided upon the purchase of a beautifully carved ivory box for Miranda when he spied, in a niche opposite the tiny window, such a thing as he had never seen before.

A little pine tree was growing in a pot, a real, living one, and a miniature of just such a tree, bent and twisted by the sea winds, that grew upon the hill above the Susquehanna at home. The art of stunting and pruning these tiny trees, developed in Japan perhaps, but known to some Chinese, was quite unheard of in the Western world so that Humphrey could scarcely believe his eyes when they told him it was green and growing and evidently kin to the giant ones in America.

"Miranda must have that," was his instant decision; "she will find that I can manage to bring home the gold snuffbox and something more besides."

His determined effort to buy the tree, however, had a strange effect. At the first the old shopkeeper merely met all his offers with a determined shake of the head, but, as Humphrey insisted, he became more and more excited and at last, wringing his hands, burst into a torrent of jabbering explanation. Captain Reynolds had cruised along these shores long enough to have learned a little of the mixed dialect of French, Spanish and Moorish words by which foreigners and natives contrived to understand one another, so that he was able to gather from the Chinaman's flood of talk that the pine tree was the most precious of his possessions, that he had carried it himself all the way from Pekin, that it was a hundred years old and that he felt certain the spirits of his ancestors loved to cluster about its twisted little branches. What had caused his banishment from his own land Humphrey could not make out, but he did gain some inkling of how the withered old man felt as he looked back upon some frail, small hut on the shore of one of China's muddy yellow rivers, upon some bit of land that he and his ancestors had tilled patiently for unnumbered generations, upon a tiny garden where the tree had grown. No, it was quite plain that he would not sell it!

So the ivory box was bought for Miranda after all. As Humphrey prepared to go, a picturesque person came into the shop, a fat, black man, very richly dressed with the silk scarfs, satin cloak and gold embroidered garments of a high court official. The young American glanced at him curiously as he squeezed by in the semi-darkness of the narrow place and was conscious of the penetrating stare of two hard black eyes that he could almost feel boring into his back as he went out. Before he had gone far, he thought that he heard a queer, smothered cry of terror in the shop. But the street was so full of noises that, though he paused to listen, he could not be certain and so went on again. In the busy days on board ship that followed, the Chinaman and his treasure presently passed completely from his mind.

Reports of the *West Wind's* quick passage had been going about, all this time, through the Mediterranean Fleet.

"But that was only a trial," Humphrey kept saying, "when we were learning how to handle her. On the voyage home we'll show you even more plainly what she can do."

That voyage was now soon to be, for the vessel had been selected to carry back the Commodore's dispatches and reports to Washington. On the day before she was to sail, a message came from the Pasha of Tripoli that he was sending his personal representative to make the ship a visit of ceremonious farewell. Captain Reynolds sighed deeply when he heard this news, for such overtures from a government elaborately friendly but secretly treacherous, were uneasy occasions. When the stout, dusky minister of state came over the side, gorgeous in his jewels and satins, Humphrey, after a moment of doubt, recognized him as the man whom he had met in the old Chinaman's shop. The other gave no sign of recognition, however, but gravely went through the elaborate messages from his august master, inspected the ship with solemn interest and expressed not only surprise, but some doubts when told of the time she had made between America and Gibraltar.

"Why, it cannot be done!" he cried. Not even pirate craft, it seemed, could fly on such swift wings. "There are favorable winds and chances for good luck on the eastern passage, but when your prow is turned toward home again, when you are obliged to go southward to get the trade winds that blow for all ships alike, then you will find that this is an ordinary craft, just like all the rest."

"We will equal our record or better it," Humphrey replied obstinately, "although, as I own, the westward voyage is a longer and more difficult one. But the *West Wind*, sir, is a ship not like other ships."

After they had sat some time in the Captain's cabin, partaking of refreshment and exchanging polite assurances of good will, the black visitor, with great ceremony, produced an impressive gift from his master, a richly embroidered scarf which he presented with a long speech that Humphrey only half understood. He accepted it unwillingly and made such reply as he could, after which there came an awkward pause in the talk. Finally the Tripolitan minister, with smooth boldness, remarked that his illustrious master would be willing to accept in return some small gift, merely as a remembrance of the visit of Captain Reynolds and his beautiful ship. For a moment Humphrey was utterly at a loss, since the Government that had filled his magazines with powder and shot in case of trouble had quite neglected to provide for any such occasion as this. Yet the beady eyes of the African, fixed so steadily upon him, seemed to hint that some present must be forthcoming or serious difficulties would follow. There seemed but one thing to do.

"How Miranda will laugh at me, after all," Humphrey sighed as he slowly brought out the gold snuffbox and placed it in the dark hand that was extended so quickly to receive it.

The exchange of gifts should have brought the visit to an end, but for some reason it did not. The African still sat, staring across the table at Humphrey, his eyes narrowed to black slits.

"The gift is of great beauty," he said at last, "but I might explain that the Pasha, my master, has especial love for his gardens and is most particularly delighted when he is given any—any small curiosity to add to the treasures he has already gathered there." Seeing Humphrey look blank, he explained more clearly. "You and I met, some days since, in the shop of that mad old Chinaman who owns, but will not sell, that little pine tree, a hundred years old. The Pasha had taken a fancy to own it, so, since the old man would not part with it willingly, he sent some servants to—to fetch it. But they failed. I understand the tree is on board this ship after all."

"On board the *West Wind*?" echoed Humphrey amazed. "I give you my word that it is not here."

"The tree is on this ship," insisted the other steadily. "The Chinaman heard somehow of our coming and departed, treasure and all; he was seen fleeing through the town; he was seen making his way to this vessel. And the Pasha of Tripoli desires the little pine tree!"

There was a pause, but Humphrey said nothing. The dusky visitor shrugged his shoulders and slipped one sleek hand within his satin robe.

"The American Captain wishes further persuasion," he said with a sly grin. "I have something here for himself alone, which will perhaps make him more generous."

He drew out a handful of gold coins and laid them upon the table, looked at Humphrey narrowly and, seeing no signs of yielding, sighed deeply and drew out another and another. He piled them up in little shining heaps and stood gazing, with an expectant smile across at the American. But, since Humphrey did not put out a hand to take them he broke forth petulantly—

"In the name of the Prophet, is not that enough? You grasping Yankees would have everything! These are not African coins, man, but good English sovereigns, French louis d'or, Spanish doubloons such as you can spend like water anywhere you go. And all in exchange for one small thing upon which my master has set his heart. Come, you drive a hard bargain."

"I drive no bargain for what does not belong to me, to be paid for in stolen coin," Humphrey answered hotly. "Do you think that I do not know that your pirate vessels have brought in this gold; that, for each of those heaps of coin, there has probably been a good ship sent to the bottom, English, French or Spanish? Have you not learned once what America thinks of piracy?"

The fat man shrugged his shoulders again.

"America is a forgetful land, and far away," he commented drily. "News carries thither slowly and judgment comes even slower back again. It is twenty years since your country fought with mine; we believe America is ceasing to watch us. The Atlantic is a broad and windy sea!"

"You do not know," the young officer replied slowly, "that there is a wise man in my country, my comrade and dear friend, who has learned how to make the Atlantic a thousand miles less broad. He built this ship with which we have shortened the voyage by four days and will, when we set sail again, lessen it by more than that. Your pirate craft are swift but Yankee wits are swifter and presently your vessels will bring back a tale—for every sea-coast will ring with it—that Jonathan Adams' ship the *West Wind* has crossed the ocean in eighteen days."

"Eighteen days," scoffed the other, "that is past any man's belief. Ships move by sails, not wings!"

"Eighteen days," repeated Humphrey sternly, "I promise you that you will hear of our voyage made in just that time. And when other vessels are built to match or to better her, our country will come a great stride nearer to you, a thousand miles nearer to traitors, murderers and thieves."

He brought his hand down upon the table with such force that the heaps of gold went rolling and tumbling to the floor, and the dignified Arab was forced to go groveling on his hands and knees to pick them up again. When he arose, Humphrey was standing by the door which he held open.

"I will send an officer," he said, "to go with you to search the ship. Since you believe that no man speaks the truth, you shall see with your own eyes that the Chinaman and his treasure are not here."

There was no doubt that the man who had the duty of escorting the foreigner over the ship took extreme delight in conducting him through the narrowest, dirtiest recesses of the hold, so that the court official's fat person was breathless and his silken garments much the worse for grease and tar when he finally expressed himself as satisfied and came once more on deck. His farewells were less stately than his greetings had been, and he turned back for a last word before he went over the side.

"If the *West Wind* sails away, after all, carrying my master's heart's desire, may every curse and every evil spirit known to good Mohammedans, follow you upon your way. May every hardship that sailors can suffer, fall upon you, may your voyage be such a one as never captain knew before!"

He departed in a great show of dignity and magnificence and was rowed ashore, while Humphrey, with a sigh of relief, turned himself to the preparations for getting under way. He had vowed a vow within himself that Jonathan Adams should not be disappointed and that, on the homeward voyage, they would shorten the passage by the five days for which he had hoped.

It was at daylight next morning, when the *West Wind* had cleared the harbor of Tripoli and, leaving behind the palm-clad shore with its minarets and towers and its evil, hostile city, was standing out to sea, that Captain Reynolds sat down in his cabin to examine the log book which he had sent for, to make certain that wind and weather and the exact hour of weighing anchor had been correctly noted. He smiled as he glanced at the entry of the day before with its record of the visit of state.

"And he had the impudence, even, to curse me," he reflected, chuckling, "as though any one could hide on my ship without my knowing—"

He stopped abruptly, the page half-turned in his hand. For a strange sound was developing in the locker opposite his bunk, a scratching as though a rat were shut in behind the door, then the clicking of the latch as, out from the narrow space where no one would think a grown man could hide, came tumbling the Chinaman, half-smothered, but clutching unharmed his heart's treasure in its porcelain pot.

The Mohammedan's curse had been thorough and, so it began to seem as the voyage went on, of some effect, but he had forgotten one thing. Whatever went wrong, whatever accident, small or great, befell the ship on her race across the Atlantic, the wind never failed. The very sprites, afreets and genie known to Arab fancy seemed to sit in the hollow of the sail and lend strength with their blowing to the lusty trade winds. Lines parted, tackle jammed, and sails carried away, but still the wind held. The oldest but ablest seaman, he who had not believed in Gibraltar when he saw it, fell from a yard and was picked up with a broken knee. A falling block, dropping from a height to the deck below, crushed, in its passage, the shoulder of another sailor. But still the wind held and still the ship cut the South-Atlantic rollers like an arrow. Seven days, eight days, nine days—they were halfway across, and excitement had begun to run breathlessly high.

At the end of the ninth day, while the *West Wind* was wallowing in a cross sea, it was discovered that the water casks had broken loose from their lashings, that two of them were crushed, others injured, and that the greater portion of their precious water had leaked away.

"Then we have need to make port all the more quickly," Captain Reynolds said grimly, and stood by in person while, to each man including himself, the meager allowance for each day was measured out.

The one who fared worst upon the voyage was the old Chinaman. He suffered hideously from sea-sickness for the first few days, although he made shift to stagger on deck, to haul at ropes and to give such service as his feeble strength allowed. When the water failed, he seemed, somehow, to be suffering far more than any of the rest. On the second day after the mishap to the casks, he came to the captain's cabin, utterly refusing to be driven away. With trembling yellow hands he drew the pine tree from beneath his rags and set it on the table.

"After I die," he requested calmly, "will you not in justice see that my share of water still goes to keeping my ancestors' tree alive?"

It seemed that his whole allowance of drinking water had been poured into the pot, since he preferred to perish himself rather than permit his great treasure to droop and wither.

Humphrey argued and commanded, but to no purpose. The Chinaman merely shook his head obstinately and vowed by all his gods that he would not drink while his tree was thirsty. At last, however, a compromise was made. The little pine was to remain on the Captain's table and every day, in Humphrey's presence, the Chinaman was to drink half his allowance of water and pour the other half upon the dry roots.

"If you can keep alive on that, your tree should also," Humphrey said; "there is no other way to do."

Still muttering protests that his tree would die, the old man crawled away. Humphrey stood looking silently at the little pine tree, so fresh and vigorous in spite of its hundred years. He took the water that had been set upon his table and drank half of it at one gulp, for he had just come below and the hot quarterdeck was a thirsty place. Then he paused a moment, the half-empty cup in his hand.

"I am a soft-hearted fool," he muttered and poured what was left on the dry earth of the porcelain pot.

The days passed while the men grew weaker and more sluggish at their work, but still the breeze held and the speed of the *West Wind* did not falter. They passed no ship from which they could obtain water, their only hope lay in the making of port. They turned northward, lost the trade winds, seemed for a terrible moment to be hanging becalmed, but a stiff breeze caught them and bore them still toward home. The old Chinaman seemed to shrivel away like a dead leaf, but he came stumbling every day to share his mouthful of water with his precious tree. Captain Reynolds himself looked more worn and haggard than did any of his men. Only the Chinaman, glancing sideways with his slanting, beady eyes at the lusty green of the little pine, seemed to suspect why. They were like the flitting ghosts of a ship's crew that morning when the hot, glittering expanse of sea was broken by a wavering line on the horizon and the lookout's husky call of "Land-ho" announced the low green shore of Maryland. Eighteen days from Gibraltar and all records broken at last!

She came into the Susquehanna River for repairs, did the worn but triumphant *West Wind*, and Jonathan Adams came rowing out to board her, his sober face for once all wreathed in smiles.

"By five days you shortened the voyage," he said, "and I had not really hoped for more than four. I always said she was not a tub, but a real ship at last. There will be others like her, and her children's children will dare to spread such sail that they will cross the Atlantic in half your time."

As Humphrey came up the ladder to where Miranda was waiting on the wharf, his first words were—

"I left the snuffbox behind," while she, laughing shakily, answered—

"I knew you would."

The whole crew, down to the cabin boy, were hailed as heroes when they left the ship, but there was one who managed somehow to go ashore as mysteriously as he had come aboard. The old Chinaman with his treasured pine tree disappeared, no one knew whither, hiding himself, perhaps, lest some emissary from Africa should even yet seek him out and rob him. For more than a month Humphrey searched and inquired for him all up and down the shore of the bay, but no one had seen him and no one knew where he had gone.

Jonathan Adams' ship the *West Wind* sailed on many voyages and was the model for other vessels of her class, bigger and swifter even than herself—the great race of American clippers that once ruled the seas. They gave our country the highest place in the world's shipping, and they brought her, even as Humphrey had said, a thousand miles nearer to her neighbors across the Atlantic. But that is not all of the story of this famous voyage. The real end came seven years later, when Humphrey had risen to be Commodore Reynolds and when, between two cruises, he was spending a holiday at home. One summer afternoon, a small, bent figure toiled up the driveway of the big house above the Susquehanna. Humphrey, with Miranda, was sitting in the shade of the high-columned veranda and for a moment did not recognize the strange face, so covered with dust that the yellow skin and slanting eyes were scarcely visible. But the old Chinaman walked straight to Miranda and laid his offering on her lap.

"For you," he said. "He wanted to bring it to you from the very first!"

It was not the real pine tree, but the one that you see here, made of jade and enamel with tiny jewels set around the top of the pot. Humphrey and his wife exclaimed and admired and examined it on every side.

"But I do not understand," Humphrey kept saying. "How did you come to make it, and to bring it to us after seven years?"

"After seven years!"

The old Chinaman smiled patiently.

"You Americans are ever in such haste. How long, think you, it takes a true craftsman to carve a tree of jade?"

CHAPTER VIII

HOBGOBLINS

Betsey and David were frankly gossiping, but with the most intent and serious purpose in the world. The days were growing so long that they could do their studying out of doors in the evenings, and the place of their choosing, where they struggled with dates and angles and difficult lines of Virgil, was the stretch of grass around the pool. When the first stars began to show in the water, it was a signal for discussion of lessons to be put aside. Later they would walk back to the cottage, where Betsey would help Miss Miranda in the kitchen or would stroll with her in the garden while David would go into the workshop, take off his coat, arm himself with an oil can in one hand and a wrench in the other and would say to Mr. Reynolds, who usually did not even hear him come in—

"All ready, sir."

To-night they were delaying a little, after having mastered the subject of extreme and mean ratio, and were piecing together such bits of knowledge as each one had concerning their friends in the white cottage, trying to come to some conclusion as to what was the matter and what could be done. Michael's doleful face seemed to give warning every day that the "feeling in his bones" was in no way diminished, and Miss Miranda appeared more and more concerned and weary.

"Miss Miranda only meant to help us remember the Barbary pirates," David was saying, "but she told us more than that. I begin to see how it is their blood, hers and her father's, to dream of progress and new things. That new engine that Mr. Reynolds is trying to develop may turn out as great a thing as the clipper ship, and may bring as many changes. And she is doing as much for it as her father, managing that he is never disturbed or troubled or discouraged. Even if he should want to give it up, I think she wouldn't let him."

"She is more like Jonathan Adams than like Humphrey Reynolds," rejoined Elizabeth, "though they were both her great-grandfathers. Jonathan's daughter married Humphrey's son and they inherited the shipyard, so she told me yesterday, and built clipper ships after him. Some of them really did sail to Europe in nine days, just as Jonathan had hoped. They made a great fortune during that time when American ships were trading with the whole world."

"And it was that fortune that built this house," David took up the thread of speculation, "and gave Mr. Reynolds his scientific education and sent him to all sorts of places abroad to study. But where is it?"

"Wherever it has gone," Betsey said, "it may come back again some day. I will always like to think of how Jonathan and Humphrey succeeded in the face of everything. I think Mr. Reynolds will succeed in the same way."

"Miss Miranda will never lose courage," David observed reflectively, "but her father is—a little different. He is old and tired and he is trying to do the work of a young man, of a person with strength and confidence in himself. Without Miss Miranda he might have lost spirit long ago, but she will help him to the very end. She is anxious and lonely, she wants her brother, and she wants her house. But more than anything she wants her father's success."

"They must have been very happy when they lived here," Betsey went on, "with Mr. Reynolds busy at his work, with Ted coming home for vacations—he was only just out of college, Michael says, when the war began—with that Cousin Donald gone into business and doing well. Mr. Reynolds must have given him the money for a start and I think they must all have felt more comfortable when he was gone. And then the house burned and the war came, and everything was changed so that nobody was happy any more."

"Mr. Reynolds is happy," David insisted; "whatever is wrong is being kept from him. To work at something you love that is coming nearer and nearer to success, that is one of the best things there is. But Miss Miranda isn't happy! And she is growing more unhappy every day. It's time something was done."

"If her brother could only come home," Betsey suggested.

"He might come home to-morrow, he might be kept a year," replied David. "No, we can't wait for him. We will have to do something ourselves."

"But what can we do?" questioned Betsey blankly.

"I don't know yet," confessed David, knitting his eyebrows in earnest thought as he sat on the grass with his arms about his knees, "but there is bound to be something we can do if we just stand by and try hard enough. And I would try anything for Miss Miranda!"

There was nothing small or mean about David's ambitions nor in the loyalty of his friendship.

"While we are talking it all over, there is one other thing I should like to speak about," began Betsey hesitatingly. "Do you ever think that there is anything about this house—this place that was a house—that is at all—queer?"

David sat bolt upright and stared at her fixedly.

"You have been talking to Michael," he accused her. "Michael says that ill luck is brooding over the whole place like a summer thunderstorm and that there is no telling where the bolt will strike. I never saw a person who could believe such strange things as Michael."

"No," Betsey maintained stoutly, "it is not from anything he said. It is only what I have seen myself."

She sat looking at him, first with sharp penetration, then with the dawn of a sudden discovery. She was possessed of less soaring ambition than David, but of a more keenly observant eye.

"You have seen something yourself," she announced. "You are trying to argue me out of it because you don't want to believe your own eyes. Tell me what you have seen."

David was silent for a minute, apparently struggling obstinately against his own convictions.

"It was just—lights, and—and something moving," he confessed shamefacedly at last. "It might have been almost anything, wind, fireflies, moonlight on that broken mirror. I'm not going to let Michael make me believe in goblins."

"It is only lately that I have seen it," Betsey said. "From the house where I live you can see the top of this hill and I am certain that, on three nights at least, I have seen a light moving back and forth among the ruins. It is very small and dim and it goes so slowly, sometimes I think it has disappeared entirely but it always comes in sight again. One night it was raining and the next the moon was shining and the next it was dim starlight, but the light was there. And you have seen it too?"

"Yes," admitted David, "though I have tried to make myself believe it was a mistake. I was coming up Somerset Lane after dark, the first time, and I saw that same light, bobbing and jerking across the broken walls. I stopped and watched and tried to persuade myself that it was fireflies or glow-worms, but I didn't succeed. A very small light, as you say, and moving slowly but never really coming to rest. I—I don't quite like it."

It was growing dusky in the shadow of the pines, so that Betsey began to look about her with a slight uneasiness. The subject was one that did not tend greatly toward making one peaceful or at rest in that lonely place.

"I rather believe Miss Miranda will be looking for us," she said somewhat lamely at last. David laughed.

"I don't feel very comfortable here myself," he agreed, "and it is getting rather dark. Yes, it must be time to go."

They went along the path together to the gate without speaking, until, with his hand on the lock, David paused and looked back.

"I am going back after it grows really dark," he said, "to see what that thing is. It ought not to go on."

"Oh, no," cried Elizabeth in real horror. "Oh, no!"

"It is something that ought to be cleared up," David insisted steadily. "If we don't do it ourselves, we should tell some one who will. The place belongs to Miss Miranda and it should be looked after. Yes, I am going to see about it to-night."

"Then," replied Elizabeth with a long and rather gasping breath, "if you will go, I am going with you."

They did not work very long at their respective tasks that evening. Betsey was an absent-minded helper as she put away the dishes and David, it appeared later, had dropped so many tools and needed to be told so many things twice over, that even Mr. Reynolds had grasped vaguely that something was not quite right and had stopped to gaze at him over his spectacles, in mild and pained astonishment. It was earlier than usual and just at the edge of real darkness, the soft, black dark of a warm spring night before the moon has risen, when David presented himself at the kitchen door for the ostensible purpose of taking Elizabeth home. With rather trembling hands she took off her apron and put away her towels, and prepared to go with him. But their plan was not to be carried out so easily, or without any hitch.

"I will walk down the hill with you," announced Miss Miranda with somewhat disconcerting suddenness. "I have some things to take to Mrs. Donovan at the foot of the lane. I promised her some of my cabbage plants."

"We will take them," chorused the two conspirators, speaking together with such promptness that any one less preoccupied than Miss Miranda might have guessed that some project was on foot.

"No, I must see her myself," she persisted and set out with them, to their ill-concealed dismay.

"It is not very late and we can come back after she has left us," David found opportunity to say before Miss Miranda joined them with the cabbage plants.

They went down the hill without much of their usual talking and laughter, for Miss Miranda appeared absorbed in her own thoughts, and her two companions, perhaps a little appalled by their undertaking, seemed to have not much to say. They bade her good-night at Mrs. Donovan's door with suspicious alacrity and, having seen it safely closed, turned once more up the lane. By David's advice they were to pass the cottage, climb higher up the hill and find the spot where the boundary wall was nearest the ruins of the house.

"If we wait by the pool," he explained, "we might not see anything. It might not come near, whatever It is."

Betsey shivered a little. She was ashamed of the thrills that were running through her and the tendency of her teeth to chatter unless she kept them firmly closed.

They walked briskly, but some one who came behind them was walking quicker still. A man passed them as they trudged upward, a man quite indistinguishable in the dark, save for the faint white of his collar and of his face. Betsey could make out that he was a broad person, not very tall, with an alert, though rather heavy step. They lagged a little after he had passed, to let him get well ahead of them so that they could go on with the discussion of their plans unheard.

"Usually it's not very late when the light comes," David said. "I don't believe we will have very long to wait."

THE POOL OF STARS

In spite of his haste, the man who had passed them must have lingered a moment at the Reynolds' gate, for he was only just opening it and going up the walk as they came by. The light from the cottage windows fell upon him as he approached the door and showed his figure more clearly although his face was still hidden. Betsey looked at him curiously but David seemed too much occupied to give him more than a passing glance. They left the lane, skirted the wall and came finally to the place they sought.

"Now," directed David, "here is a broken tree leaning against the wall. Up you go."

With a little assistance and not much scrambling, she clambered to the top of the wall. They were at the back of the house here, with the nearest line of blackened ruin not a hundred feet away. A spreading willow grew so close to the wall that its feathery boughs brushed Elizabeth's hair and passed smooth fingers across her cheek. The stones were warm under their hands, from the past day's sun, their heads were among the leaves and birds' nests, very high, it seemed, above the ground. The whole desolate place before them was very still.

"The moon will be up presently," David whispered, "so I think It will come soon, while it is still dark."

Betsey trembled a little in the warm night air, but said nothing. The minutes passed, then a half hour, finally the hour itself struck from a spire in the village. The strokes sounded very thin and far away as the night wind carried them. A faint cow bell jingled in a distant field, a comfortable, friendly sound that Elizabeth missed when it moved and died away. They began to relax their tense muscles as the time passed slowly, to swing their feet and to talk almost above their breath.

"It may not be coming to-night," said David, "we will not wait much longer."

"That man at the Reynolds' gate, I wonder what he wanted," observed Betsey. "It was rather late for just ordinary visitors. Did you notice him, David?"

"When the light fell on him I thought I had seen him before," he answered. "Yet after all it was no one I knew, just a man I saw in the village this morning by the post office."

Elizabeth was not greatly heeding, for the round, golden rim of the moon was showing almost opposite them, above the jagged heaps of ruins. Slowly it rose, spreading more light through the trees, until it was half above the horizon and shone, an orange semicircle, there above the old house. She was about to speak when David touched her elbow.

"Look beyond that pine tree," he whispered.

The little glow-worm light was visible at last. It was, at first, half hidden by the bushes, but it moved slowly along, swinging near the ground, hesitating, almost coming to a standstill, but still always making some progress. It moved along the ruined walls, it came nearer and nearer. To both of them it became evident that whatever it was, whatever carried it, must presently pass opposite them and be darkly outlined against the glowing background of the moon. They had only to wait and they would see.

The wait, however, began to seem very long, since the wavering advance of the point of light was very slow. Betsey, in the lagging delay as the seconds passed, felt her attention beginning to wander. She noticed how slim and graceful were the sweeping boughs of the tree that hid them, she observed the thin frettings of black and white of the shadows of the leaves on the wall. Very earnestly she wished that she could sit as still as David could and not be tempted to swing her feet against the stones. She began to think, as the minutes still dragged, of that man they had seen go in at Miss Miranda's gate.

"David," she leaned over to whisper, "you said you had seen that man before. What did he look like?"

"Why," David answered, coming out of his own thoughts with a start, "he was dark, rather heavy, but with a thin face. I didn't like him."

"Did he have," a slow possibility was dawning in Betsey's mind, as she dwelt upon who this man might be, why he had come, and as she recollected a chance phrase spoken by the farmer's wife beside the river, "did he have a sharp, selfish face?"

"Why, I think so." David spoke so very slowly that she could have shaken him for his deliberation. "Yes, I rather think he did. He had scowling black eyebrows and eyes very close together. Yes, I would put it just that way myself, a sharp, selfish face."

That was the way Mrs. Bassett had put it, and Michael also. Elizabeth swung her feet over to the other side of the wall, the weird, moving light quite forgotten.

"I am going back," she said. "It must be that cousin, Donald Reynolds. I do believe he was waiting in the lane for Miss Miranda to go out, so that he could find her father alone. And she has always dreaded his coming. Oh, why didn't we think who it was before!"

"But—but—" stammered David, quite dazed.

One more minute and that hidden figure would move across the moon, but she had no thought for that mystery now. She jumped down outside the wall and ran, ran with all breathless speed, stumbling in the thick grass and over jutting roots and stones until she came out at last into the moonlit lane. Her heart was thumping against her side and Miss Miranda's gate looked very far. She sped down the hill with no further thought of what she and David had gone out to find; it was no time to be spying on goblins when this much-dreaded and very real person was so near.

CHAPTER IX

THE SUBSTANCE OF A DREAM

Scarcely even for a passing glance did Elizabeth pause at the front door of the cottage although it stood open, as Miss Miranda had left it, with the lamp still burning cheerfully on her sewing table inside. Weary and breathless, she stumbled along the path, turned the corner of the house, and saw the brightly lighted workshop with its door also standing open to the warmth of the night. It was as she thought, the stranger was here, sitting on the high stool beside the table, talking volubly, thrusting forward his long-chinned, dark face and pounding on his knee to give emphasis to what he said. Mr. Reynolds sat opposite in the one arm chair the place afforded, looking white and frail and old in contrast to his visitor, very quiet, and listening with earnest attention. Like an image of carved ebony, Dick sat immovable on one of the posts of the back of the chair. The green-shaded light, with its brilliant, narrow circle of illumination, showed nothing else clearly, but gave only faint vision of wheels and pulleys, of shining glints that sparkled back from polished steel or ruddy copper, while through the whole room droned the slow song of turning wheels.

There was a step on the flagstones behind Elizabeth just before she mounted the doorstep. As she had hoped, David had followed her. Both men glanced up as the boy and girl entered, but there was no pause in the talk, since any new presence seemed to make no impression on the tenseness of the scene. Even Dick scarcely turned his head as he sat like some brooding spirit above his master.

"Can't you stop those infernal wheels?" Donald Reynolds said, as they came in. "I cannot hear my own voice with them grinding away in my ears."

"David!" said the older man in tone of request.

With quick obedience, David stepped to the end of the room, pulled a lever, jerked a protesting, crackling switch and brought the whirring song to an end. Without the familiar sound the place seemed uncannily silent as Donald went on talking. To the presence of David and Betsey he gave no heed, having apparently but one thought, to speak the words he had come to say before Miss Miranda should return.

"So I made up my mind that you should be told what a great wrong you are doing Miranda," he resumed. "For ten years you have spent time and money on this worthless piece of work, pottering and tinkering and pretending that you really hoped to accomplish something in the end."

"But I have accomplished something," returned the old man gravely. "I am very near to success now and ten years is not long when you remember that I lost all my records and all my models when the house was burned. No, ten years has not been too much to spend."

"It is not time alone that you have spent, but money, spent it like water when it should have been making Miranda comfortable. Have you stopped, ever, to think of how she works and saves and pinches, how she toils in that garden and fattens miserable fowls for the market so that you can go on with this game of yours?"

"Miranda chose to have it so," Mr. Reynolds returned quietly, but the two onlookers could see him wince.

"Have you known Miranda longer than any of us and have not yet learned that she would give the breath out of her body to make other people happy? Would she complain or choose otherwise if she thought your desire was set upon this one thing, this machine that you call a life work, but that any one else would call a pleasant fad, a plaything that would never succeed?"

"If my recollection is correct," Mr. Reynolds said, "she used to make some sacrifices for you, when you lived with us, that you might be happy."

His chance shot seemed to strike at some more vivid memory than he knew. The other was silent for a minute, but then burst forth again, more sharply and bitterly than before.

"Is that any reason why I should stand by now, and see her robbed and cheated as you are cheating her? You are willing to spend your life following a dream, but you have no right to spend hers. You say that she is willing, but do you really know it? Do you notice how worn and tired and anxious she begins to look?"

Elizabeth would have broken in upon him, checking his words with a wild tumult of indignant protest, but David laid a hand upon her arm. This was a matter for their elders alone, his look seemed to say, and must not be interrupted.

"Suppose, Donald," Mr. Reynolds was beginning gently, "suppose this affair were to turn out less of a dream than you think? We have followed dreams before, we and our forbears in this family, and they have led to success and—what appeals to you far more—to fortune. Miranda is, I know, looking worn and troubled; I think it is her home that she is grieving for. It is my belief that in a very little time she may have it back again."

"People like you are always hopeful," returned Donald, "always declaring that with a little more time and a great deal more money, success will come. Can you not stop deceiving yourself, can you not give up and admit that you have failed? You have a handful of screws and wires and a few turning wheels here—" he waved his hand to include the whole workshop in the scorn of a person who knows nothing of mechanics—"but what do they signify? What do they count for compared to ten years of your life, or of Miranda's?"

He leaned his elbows on the table, brought his face closer yet to his unhappy uncle's and spoke with even fiercer accusation.

"You say that you will be able to give back to Miranda the house she loves, when all that you have ever done is to destroy it for her. Have you ever looked over the ruins, as I have, noticed that the blaze was hottest at the south end, and hottest of all where your workshop stood? That was where the fire began, there can be no doubt of it. Miranda says it was lightning that set the house on fire, but—" he lowered his voice—"I know better. A spark from one of your wires, a blaze in some oily packing, that is what brought about the tragedy. You mechanical geniuses are too much in the clouds to safeguard those you pretend to love. The burning of the house was due to your own heedlessness!"

"No, no, Donald," cried the old man, driven out of his calmness at last, and with his voice betraying cruel pain. "I can't—I won't believe that it was my doing!"

"You may be certain that it was," returned the other without mercy, "and I think, in your inmost heart, you have long suspected that it was so."

Betsey was no longer to be silenced, not even by David's insistent pressure on her arm.

"It's not true," she burst out. "We saw ourselves where the lightning struck, that began the fire. The chimney was split from top to bottom."

"Yes?" assented Donald, turning to her and speaking in a tone of hard, cold quiet. "You can prove that, I suppose? You can show the marks to my uncle here? Real evidence would comfort him greatly."

"No—no," she faltered in reply. "We were exploring in the ruins and some of the walls fell. The marks of the lightning don't show now. But we both saw them."

"I will hold to my own opinion still," answered Donald Reynolds, "and my uncle, though he would like to, will not be able to disagree with me. Isn't it—hullo, there's something wrong with the old man."

For Mr. Reynolds was leaning back in his chair with his eyes closed, unmoving and unhearing. Betsey ran to his side and took up one of his hands. It was limp and lifeless, although she could feel the faint pulse still beating. Donald, in evident concern, was coming closer, but David barred the way and warned him off.

"You are an impudent pair of young ones," exclaimed Donald. "Who are you and what is your business here, anyway?"

"We are friends of Miss Miranda's," Betsey explained briefly. "I think you have done her father some very great harm."

"I thought it was only my duty to say a word or two to put things right," the man answered. "It is not fair to Miranda that no one should tell her father the truth."

"You did not speak one word of truth," returned David heatedly. "You guessed about the burning of the house and you guessed wrong. And you did not even guess about the invention. You know as much of mechanical things as—as Dick does."

"I am a practical man," Donald Reynolds said, "and I have no patience with toys and dreams."

He spoke with less bluster than was to be expected, for he seemed truly disturbed by the evident harm he had brought about. His words roused his uncle from the lethargy into which he had fallen for the old man spoke suddenly and very clearly.

"There are many idle dreams and some true ones," he said, "and it is only through the true dreams that the world goes forward."

Then he closed his eyes once more, drew a long sigh and sank lower in the chair. Donald Reynolds stood irresolute, troubled but unconvinced and ready to argue his case still.

"You had better go," Betsey had the courage to tell him with blunt plainness. "Mr. Reynolds will be better when you are out of sight. There's no use in your waiting to talk to Miss Miranda."

Donald Reynolds, it seemed, thought the same thing. He took up his hat, began to say something, perhaps in apology or excuse for what he had done, made such small success of it that he gave up the attempt, and turned to the door. The two beside Mr. Reynolds paid little attention to his going, only Dick hailed his departure with a defiant caw.

"I suppose he is telling himself that he has acted for the best," commented David bitterly. "At least he has sense enough to seem a little sorry for what he has done."

"I see now why Miss Miranda has looked so worried," Betsey added. "She has been afraid he would come here and say just such cruel, untrue things."

When David had brought a glass of water for Mr. Reynolds and Betsey had propped him up with cushions, he seemed to feel better, although still to be rather dazed.

"Did he mean it? Was he right?" he questioned them pitifully, looking across at his well-beloved wheels hanging in idleness. "Have I really been so blind and selfish as to do Miranda such great wrong?"

It seemed a long wait before they heard her step outside.

"Go to meet her, tell her that—that nothing is wrong," he directed. "Do not let her be anxious. I am sure you can explain it all."

David stayed by his side while Betsey went to tell what had happened. It was not easy, especially after she saw the look of alarm that came into her friend's face the moment she heard that Donald Reynolds had been there. She listened quietly, however to all that Betsey had to tell.

"Oh, why was I away!" she exclaimed at the end, but it was her only lamentation. "He can say very hard and cruel things," she added; "you have not told me all of them, but I can guess."

She went to the workshop to speak to her father, but David met her at the door.

"He feels better," the boy reported, "but he said he would like to be by himself a little. He is up and walking about; I really think he will be happier if he is left alone."

They peeped in at the door and saw that Mr. Reynolds was, as David had said, standing at the bench, busy as ever, with a tool in his hand. He was handling the wrench awkwardly, as though his fingers had not much strength, but he appeared intent and absorbed, almost himself again.

Elizabeth, nevertheless, was not satisfied. She could not believe that any one so stricken as had been Mr. Reynolds an hour before, could have really recovered so quickly. Rather shyly she suggested that she should stay all night, "just so that you will not be all alone, if he should be ill again," as she told Miss Miranda, and, on her friend's relieved acceptance of the suggestion, was glad that she had offered. David went across the hill to get the things that she had telephoned to Anna to pack, while Betsey mounted the stairs with Miss Miranda to prepare a sleeping place.

"We have so few guests that I have no regular spare bedroom," her hostess explained. "If you do not mind, you will have to sleep on the couch here beside the toy-cupboard."

Later, as she went to and fro about the house, Elizabeth peeped in more than once to see how Mr. Reynolds was faring in the workshop. She stood at the door, not daring to speak or to disturb him, so busy did he seem. His face looked white, deeply lined and very tired; never had he appeared to her so really old. He was toiling very earnestly so that she felt sure he must be gaining some comfort from his work. Once, however, when she looked in she did not see him. The far corners of the room were so very dim that he might be there among the shadows, but she did not like to go in to make sure. Miss Miranda called her for something at that moment and kept her longer than she expected. Later, when she went back to make sure of his absence before she mentioned it, she saw that he was at work again by the bench and she began to believe that she must have been mistaken. He was standing beneath the light, putting away a great array of tools in a drawer.

David, returning from his errand, came whistling up to the door.

"Are you sure you do not need a doctor?" he inquired anxiously.

Miss Miranda was certain that a doctor would only disturb and upset her father. She had broached the subject to him earlier and had found the idea so distressed him, that she had given it up.

"I met Michael when I came through the garden," David told Betsey, "and when I let him know what had happened he seemed dreadfully upset. He just sat down on the bench and groaned out, 'I knew that fellow would be coming here to make some mischief, but I never knew quite what it would be. And with me watching and watching for him, he slipped in just the same. I was certain just some such unlucky thing would happen, I have been feeling it this long time back.' Poor Michael, he will probably be saying charms and repeating spells for good luck all night now."

"Did you stay long enough on the wall to—to see anything?" Betsey asked hesitatingly.

"No," he answered, "I waited minute after minute, but the Thing was so slow, and what you said had worried me too, so in the end I came away. I will have to try again."

It was very late, so that David, after some lingering and wishing that he could be of service, took his leave, Betsey walking with him as far as the gate. Here, in the moonlight they came upon Michael, sitting on a three-legged stool, his pipe in his hand and the collar of his worn coat turned up against the dews of the spring night.

"It is best that I should just wait here for a while," he explained. "I heard a step in the lane and was afraid that blackguard might be back again. Ah, what did I tell you?"

For a figure had come into the moonlit open and Donald Reynolds had laid a hand on the gate.

"You will not be entering here, sir," declared Michael severely. "You have lived up, this night, to what I always thought of you, but you have had your fling and done your work and that has been enough."

Donald shrugged his shoulders.

"You seem to have the place well guarded," he responded, "and I only came back for one thing. They gave me some letters at the post office for my uncle when I was getting my own, earlier in the day. Somehow I forgot to leave them, so, when I found them in my pocket, I brought them back rather than have a delay on my conscience. I will be going away early in the morning."

He gave the letters to Elizabeth, who took them mechanically.

"And—and how is my uncle now?" he asked hesitatingly; "if I had only known—if there is anything I can do—"

"You were always a cruel one with your tongue, Mr. Donald," Michael interrupted him drily, "and you should have learned by now that where words have hurt, words cannot heal. It is against the nature of things."

"I see, Michael, that you are the same stiff-necked old bigot still," returned the other. "Do you remember how Ted and I caught you burning three feathers of the black cock's tail on Midsummer Eve, to keep off bad luck for the year? Do you do such things still?"

"To burn the whole black cock would not lift the ill luck falling on the house that shelters you," retorted Michael hotly, "and if I do such things still it is no concern of yours. But you will not be entering this gate. Good night, sir."

The hint was so firm a one that Donald Reynolds argued no further but turned away and strode out of sight into the darkness. David was about to go through the gate and follow him down the lane, when Michael stopped him.

"Go up and look at Mr. Reynolds again before you go," he begged. "I have a feeling that all is not well with him, even yet."

"You have so many feelings, Michael, how do you know what they mean?" inquired David with interest.

The old man seated himself on his stool once more and began filling his pipe.

"Men of Ireland are not quite like the rest of the world," he said slowly. "We do not often say so, but I think it is in the hearts of all of us to think that since our fathers' fathers knew the Little People, we of their blood can feel a little deeper and see some things a little clearer than others. You wouldn't understand, not either of you, though you have keen, kind eyes yourselves."

Betsey looked back at him anxiously as they went toward the house to fulfill his request. He was lighting his pipe, the glow of the match shining picturesquely on his battered features and mild blue eyes.

"He is too old to sit there in the damp and the dark," she said, "and I am afraid he will stay in that one spot all night. But I suppose there is no use in trying to persuade him not to."

Yes, it was quite possible that Michael would sit there all night in faithful guardianship of the people he loved. He would have many quaint thoughts for company so that the time would not be dull, he would have memories of those wide, free plains and towering mountains where he once was lonely lord of thousands of sheep, memories of those giant, white-coated dogs that sped to his rescue on the night that Ted Reynolds had saved him and won his devoted service for all time. But it was more likely that his thoughts would wander farther yet, that it was fairy hounds and fairy hills that his mind's eye would see, magic rings and dancing leprechauns and many another thing that only Michael's kind can know. So clear would be his vision—as he grew a little drowsy—that the very flowers and hedges about him would seem crowded with tiny, rustling figures and the warm night air be full of the beat of little wings. For such a person as Michael, no night spent in the garden could be really dull.

As David and Elizabeth came to the workshop door they were startled by a rush and flutter of black feathers as Dick came flying out in great excitement. Yet, within, the place seemed more peaceful than ever. Mr. Reynolds had ceased his work and was sitting at the table, a place once littered inches deep with papers and tools, but now swept bare and clean. His hands lay idly before him and he sat staring, although it seemed he saw only the blank wall opposite. Again it struck Betsey how unnatural was the silence when those busy, familiar wheels stood still. He looked up at them strangely when they came in and said almost the same words he had spoken before, his voice steady but unnaturally loud.

"It is through the true dreams that the world goes forward."

Then after a moment's pause he added—

"And I have always said that a man could know a true dream from a false one, could be sure when he was working for a great good and not for a play-thing and a failure. But I was wrong—all wrong! Those wheels shall never turn again."

His head dropped suddenly on his arm and rested upon the table. Then his whole body slipped forward and would have fallen had not David caught him.

CHAPTER X

THE TOY CUPBOARD

There could be no doubt that Mr. Reynolds was very ill. A white-uniformed nurse was installed at the cottage, the doctor came daily, looking ever graver and graver, while there were worried wrinkles in Miss Miranda's forehead and she began to look very thin and white. Mrs. Bassett, the farmer's wife, coming over to pay her promised visit and finding her dear friend in such trouble, arranged hastily that some one else should take care of her own household and installed herself in the kitchen so that Miss Miranda should be free to wait upon her father. The old man lay, for the greater part of the time, in a dull stupor, waking only now and again to partial consciousness.

Elizabeth and David gave all the help that they could, but it seemed that there was little to be done. Many nights Betsey spent at the cottage when she guessed that Miss Miranda felt lonely and depressed, although her friend's cheerful spirit would never admit failing courage.

"He will be better to-morrow," she would keep saying when it was found impossible to declare that he was better to-day.

Betsey had another burden on her mind, the close approach of her college examinations. She happened to be of the sort that takes examinations with difficulty, that cannot keep from worry, excitement and misgivings beforehand. David's, of course, were coming also, and were far more formidable than hers. The Scientific School which he was entering had rigid requirements and offered a test of knowledge in which not even the boy's native wit and his hard study could be certain of success. There had been so many ups and downs in his education, he had worked with so little guidance, that there was no denying that the odds were against him. He said little of his worries, however, merely toiled away as the day came ever nearer.

He and Elizabeth were apt to sit on the doorstep of the cottage to do their lessons during these long spring evenings that were beginning to change to summer ones. One reason for their doing so was that Miss Miranda liked to have them near, but it was not to be denied that there was another one. Neither one of them said much of that strange light that they had seen moving about the ruins of the old house, but both had clear remembrance of it and, until they had opportunity to investigate it thoroughly, had no special desire to sit at dusk beside the starry pool.

Miss Miranda came out one evening to talk with them on the stone step and to hear how their work was faring. When questioned about her father she was still able to answer cheerfully, although it was plain that it cost some effort to do so.

"The doctor says that he may be ill a long time," she said at last. "He had been working hard, too hard for any one who is so old, and for the last few months, when he came near to the end of his experiments, he had been under the pressure of great excitement. And I think, though he would never say so, that sometimes the very weariness and suspense made him wonder if the invention was to be a success. I know that he had written to one of his scientific friends, the chief mechanical engineer for a great construction company, to come and inspect the new machine and that he was more disappointed than he could quite hide, that there had been no answer. He used to ask me several times a day about the letters. So when Donald came—"

The mention of letters had brought to Betsey such a sudden recollection that she interrupted.

"There were some letters that night; your cousin brought them, and they were never opened. Perhaps one of them is what your father hoped for. I think they are still lying on the table in his shop."

She sped away to fetch them with great eagerness and came back with the handful of correspondence, much of it evidently mere advertisements, but with one slim envelope that had possibilities. There was no chance that the stricken man upstairs could read it, so that Miss Miranda, without hesitation, tore the envelope open. Betsey and David watched her face intently as she read.

"It is what he wished for," she told them when she had finished. "Mr. Garven, the man to whom he wrote, seems to be much interested and even excited about the new machine, for he says that the gas turbine principle is one over which many people have been working, but no one with any success. He says that he will come to see it at any time that my father appoints." She refolded the letter slowly. "It is rather bitter," she added, with a trifle of a catch in the voice that had been so brave and steady until now, "rather bitter that this should have come by Donald's hand and just too late!"

"But it is not too late," Betsey protested with vehemence. "David can show this man the machine, he has helped your father and knows just how it should run. And I am sure that the news that the invention has been tested and proved a success would help to make Mr. Reynolds well again. Oh, do try it—do try it."

She was bouncing up and down on the doorstep in her enthusiasm over the plan. To her great delight David supported the idea heartily.

"There is no reason why any one who knows about such things should not see in a moment that the machine is a success," he declared. "And it would surely do all of us good to find that your cousin was wrong."

"It might be so," Miss Miranda agreed slowly. Elizabeth and David could actually hear the rising hope in her voice. "We can at least try. Oh, if it could only mean that things could right themselves at last!"

A telegram was dispatched by David that very night and an anxious period of waiting was spent thereafter at the white cottage.

"He is to come on Monday afternoon, that's the day before our examinations begin," Betsey told David when the final message from Mr. Garven had been received. She was so openly excited and impatient that it seemed impossible to endure quietly the slow passing of four days.

"It will help us to forget the examinations are so near," returned David.

He was not often willing to admit his reluctance to see approach that day when he was to try his fate, but it was plain that he could not think of it with much pleasure or confidence. It meant too much to him, and the obstacles to his proper preparation had been too great.

Monday came, Monday morning, seeming to be divided by the space of a year from Monday afternoon. Even Miss Miranda was openly nervous and as for Betsey, she could scarcely contain herself in her agony of suspense. If the scientist who was coming could actually pronounce the invention a success it would mean not only the remedying of present troubles that lay heavy on the household, but it would mark the end of a long period of struggle, self-denial and alternations of hope and discouragement.

David met Mr. Garven at the train, with the two assistants who had come with him, for this examination of a new invention, produced by a man of the reputation and skill of Mr. Reynolds, was no small thing. Betsey scanned them anxiously as they entered the house and observed that Mr.

Garven was gray-haired, with a clever, alert face, possibly the same age as Miss Miranda's father, but with more of briskness and vigor. The time seemed endless to her as they sat talking to their hostess in the living room, but in reality it was brief, for it was plainly the wish of every one that the business in hand be reached at once.

Miss Miranda was very quiet, but Elizabeth could see that her hand trembled as she opened the door of the shop.

"David will show you everything," she told them. It was evident that she spoke briefly because she was too nervous to say more. She and Elizabeth lingered by the door while David led the visitors forward.

For the first time Betsey noticed the unusual order of the place. Always before, when Mr. Reynolds and David worked there, the shelves and benches had been covered with tools and drawings and the table piled with papers. She knew that no person had recently put the room to rights, for no one, not even David, dared move anything for fear of misplacing it. Yet now the shop was so bare and tidy that it seemed Mr. Reynolds himself must have set things in final order, meaning truly never to work there again.

Along the walls were ranged the earlier machines from which the great idea had developed, while at the far end of the room stood the final model, the perfected dream of ten years' toil. It was the same one that had run wild and attempted to ruin itself on that day when Betsey and David came to the rescue. The strangers bent over it examining every crank and bolt with silent, intent interest. There was nothing said for a long time. It was one of the assistants who, bursting out at last, broke the silence.

"I always knew Reynolds would have it on the rest of us," he exclaimed delightedly, laughing out loud in sheer pleasure at the greatness of the achievement. "We all said that he had not disappeared from view like this for nothing. And now he has done what every one of us would have given his eyes to accomplish!"

"Yes," assented the older man slowly, "it is the principle that we have all dreamed of, that only a very great and a very patient man could bring to reality at last. Now," to David, "we will see it in motion if you please, sir."

It is probable that all in the room held their breaths as David laid his hand upon the lever. Betsey was certain that she held hers and that she felt all dry and hollow inside, so tense was her anxiety. She listened for the familiar sound of turning wheels, the smooth rising note as they spun into motion. Every one listened—but the machine remained silent.

"There is something wrong, sir," she heard David say huskily.

"Perhaps you have not thrown the proper switch," Garven suggested, but the boy shook his head miserably.

"I have started it a hundred times," he answered; "there was never anything simpler. No, the machine is not as it used to be. There must be some parts missing."

They went over it minutely, inch by inch, all four of them, while Betsey and Miss Miranda still waited by the door.

"Certain parts have been taken out," David declared at last, "the jets are missing and these valves have been unscrewed. The machine can never go without them."

There followed a search in every drawer, on every shelf, in each nook and cranny of the whole room.

"He seems to have put them away in some very safe place," an assistant said. "It is unfortunate that he did not think that some one else might wish to use them without him. Very unfortunate and very strange."

David was standing in the middle of the room, his eye on the table, once such a litter of papers but now quite bare.

"He has burned all his drawings and plans," he observed, "and he must have destroyed those missing parts. Do you remember, Betsey, he said the machine should never run again!"

"But why, why?" demanded Garven. "This is a thing I do not understand at all."

They told him the whole story, there seemed no reason for concealment. The older man heard it through in silence.

"We worked together years ago, Reynolds and I," he said at the conclusion, "and he was the same as now, very ambitious, very tenacious of his purpose, but sometimes overwhelmed with such tempests of discouragement that he would wish to destroy all that he had done. He was worn out, I knew, his letter to me showed that, and he had a hard and a cruel blow. He has brought us to the edge of a very great discovery—and has left us there?"

"Is he so ill, Miss Reynolds, that he cannot be asked where the missing parts are?" questioned one of the other men. "Surely if he knew that his friend was here, he would want to have them produced. Could you not ask him?"

"He is half-conscious at times," Miss Miranda answered doubtfully; "I might try."

"I urge you to do so," Garven said gravely. "What he has here, if it can be proved a success should mean a fortune to him, it should mean fame and, most of all, it should mean a great step forward in men's knowledge. I think nothing should be left untried."

Miss Miranda went out reluctantly; Betsey could hear her hesitating feet upon the stairs, could hear the door open above and the low sound of consultation with the nurse. There was a long pause. One man sat down, openly fidgeting and nervous, the other stood twisting and untwisting a piece of wire between his fingers. Garven was staring silently out through the window. David still stood by the machine, his back to the others, neither moving nor speaking. It was a long, tense wait for them all. It was because Dick had been banished for the afternoon, Betsey thought, that the workshop seemed so unnaturally still without him and without those ever-moving wheels. After what seemed an endless time they heard Miss Miranda coming back.

Every face turned, even David wheeled about, but a single glance showed the result of her errand.

"He roused himself a little," she said; "he seemed to understand that you were here and to be trying to remember. And then he began to wander, he talked vaguely of water and stars and that was all. It is of no use."

They shook hands at last and went away, those three men who had brought such hope with them and could leave so little behind.

"I will be in the neighborhood for a few days," Garven said as he bade Miss Miranda good-by. "If there is anything I can do for you, my dear, be sure to send for me. And if he should remember—"

"No," she returned, shaking her head, "I will not hope any longer. We have tried and failed and the affair must be forgotten. It is all over."

David went away with them to the train and Miss Miranda returned to her father. Betsey stood at the door, watching as long as she could as they went down the hill.

"Oh, dear," she sighed out loud at last, "oh, dear!"

Hope had been so high that morning and now it was quite dead. There came also over her a sudden cold memory of something she had been glad to forget. To-morrow were the examinations!

She wandered disconsolately about the house, finding it very empty. Michael was not in the garden, Mrs. Bassett had gone on some errand, so that even the kitchen was tenantless and quite silent save for the clock ticking on the wall. She sighed again as she glanced up at it.

"Such a long day," she lamented, "and there are hours of it left!"

Very slowly she went upstairs at last. She did not wish to disturb Miss Miranda, but she was too miserable and lonely to stay longer by herself. The sick-room door was open as she stole past, so that she could see within the nurse alone beside the bed. Miss Miranda must be in the sitting room, busy with her knitting or some work that would comfort her a little.

But Miss Miranda was not knitting. She was seated before the old mahogany desk as Betsey entered, she had opened the glass doors wide and was setting the whole contents of the shelves on the flat space before her.

"I was hoping you would soon come upstairs," she said to Elizabeth. "Have I ever shown you this silver ball that came from India or told you the story that was brought with it?"

Betsey was never to forget that afternoon. Treasure after treasure Miss Miranda set before her, tale after tale she told, that carried her listener so far away that trouble, disappointment, misgivings for the morrow, were all forgotten. There were stories of strange foreign lands where seafaring Reynolds forbears had journeyed to find endless adventures and to bring home tales of the glittering, colorful Orient. There were stories of her own youth, of her brother's absurd mishaps and deeds of daring, stories of the Northern woods where they had camped, of tramping journeys they had taken together over forested hills and marshy valleys, where moose called at twilight and deer broke cover as they came near. The hours sped, the hot sunlight moved across the room, touched the ceiling and was gone, the hard day was over. The nurse came to the door and said that Mr. Reynolds was better, was conscious and was asking for his daughter.

"Miss Miranda," said Betsey as, a little later they were returning the ornaments to the shelves where they belonged, "it was I that should have comforted you to-day, but you helped me instead. I don't understand how you know such wonderful things to tell, or have such strange treasures in your toy-cupboard."

Miss Miranda smiled. She seemed quite brave and cheerful again.

"People all have toy-cupboards," she answered, "hidden away somewhere in their hearts and minds. There are many who keep them always locked, store their memories and treasures there and never look at them again. But I think you should keep the doors open and, when things go wrong, when you are tired and discouraged and your spirit fails, you should take out your treasures and go over the beautiful things of the past and let yourself see again the quaint and curious and happy things that your life has held. If you do that I think you can never be quite unhappy, never can quite lose courage, never really grow old."

CHAPTER XI

RUNNING WATER

It was a thrush, singing in the early morning rain, that awakened Betsey next day. She had slept at the cottage, on the couch beside the toy-cupboard and had seen through the window, as she dropped asleep, the sky all bright with stars and had thought vaguely of how they must be shining in the pool. Through her dreams, however, she had heard, toward the dawn, the patter of rain on the sloping roof above her head and she had remembered how dry the grass was growing and how thirsty the garden, and had smiled to hear it fall. The thrush seemed to be glad also, for he sat just opposite her window, hidden among the wet leaves, and singing with all his soul to greet the gray morning. She got up and knelt by the casement to watch him, while he, too intent upon his trills and warbles and flute-like runs, seemed to pay no heed to the fact that some one was peering at him over the sill. When he had finished and flown away, when the cool rain had ceased and the sun was beginning to send long rays into the dripping garden, she remembered for the first time that this was the long-dreaded day, the morning of the examinations.

For some reason that she could not explain, she no longer minded the thought at all. The events of the day before had seemed to clear her mind, to drive the cobwebs from her brain, to give her courage. David, she knew, when there was nothing more he could do in preparation, had begun to look forward to the occasion since the very fact that the chances were against him lent some excitement to the affair. What he did know he had mastered well, but did he know the right things? He had reached a point where he was quite on edge to find out. It was necessary for him to take his examinations at the college itself, so that he would be gone for the three days that they lasted and would not see Betsey again until the trials of both of them were over. As she dressed and went downstairs she was so busy wishing him luck that she had little time to think of herself.

After all her nervous worry, she was astonished at her present calm, that lasted even while she sat in the big quiet school room with fifty others, waiting for questions to be distributed. The one thought that kept going through her head, oddly enough, was, "I am so glad I did not go with Aunt Susan!" The paper was handed to her, Plane and Solid Geometry, the most difficult subject first as it should be. She smiled joyfully as she saw, like the face of an old friend looking up at her, the question concerning the frustum of a pyramid.

It was three days later and the last of the trial was over. Elizabeth had felt unexcited throughout, but now was beginning to seem a little jaded, as though the pouring out of so much knowledge had left her limp and empty. She had not seen much of Miss Miranda, so full had the days been, merely contenting herself with telephoning or consulting with Mrs. Bassett at the kitchen door. But now she was climbing the hill again, with none too energetic feet, to be sure, and rather a dull and vacant head, but with a heart lightened of a very definite burden. She could not know her exact standing for some days, but she had, she admitted to herself frankly, no great doubt as to the result. Nothing had seemed very difficult, for steady and conscientious labor had proved its value at last. She felt rather more concerned about David. His work, also, would be finished to-day, so that she might hope to see him at the cottage that evening.

A telegraph messenger passed her, coasting joyously down the hill on his bicycle as she was toiling upward. At the gate she found Michael, the yellow dispatch still in his hand.

"I'm going in, shall I take it to Miss Miranda?" she said, but the old Irishman shook his head.

"It is for me," he answered, and, as though to prove it, turned the envelope so that she could see the address, "Mr. Michael Martin, Somerset Lane."

Michael somehow seemed rather an unexpected person to be receiving telegrams, but he was in one of his silent moods, unfortunately, and did not offer to tell his news.

"I am needing help in the garden," was all he condescended to say as he pocketed the envelope; "could you give me a hand with pulling the lettuce? Miss Miranda has not been able to come inside the place for a week."

"I'll just go in and speak to her first," Elizabeth said, a remark that seemed to displease him greatly.

"As you will," he returned, shrugging his shoulders grumpily, "but it will be dark before long and plenty of time for visiting then. It will be black darkness, too, for there is no moon now."

With a sigh Betsey agreed that he was probably right and that he should, at any rate, be humored. The garden did indeed look neglected and in want of the care Miss Miranda was accustomed to give it. The very hens and ducks seemed to be moping and less cheerful in their clucks and quackings, as though they missed their mistress and found the unsympathetic Michael a very sorry substitute. When Betsey was once established between the lettuce rows he went away at once to hoe the sweet corn, so that conversation was impossible.

THE POOL OF STARS

They labored in silence for a long time until it began to grow too dark to see clearly.

"I will not stop before he does," Betsey told herself, rather nettled at his uncordial behavior; "he will think I am shirking if I do."

The fresh green lettuce heads had grown huge and compact like gigantic roses and filled, heaping full, the big basket he had set beside her. She went on thinning them out, pulling chance weeds, clipping the long stalks, determined to make no move until the unapproachable Michael suggested it. She thought much of David as she worked there in the dusk. Had he done well or had chance gone against him? Would he come soon to report how things were or would his return be so late that she would have to wait until morning to hear how he had fared? With a little good luck he should have got through famously but, somehow, good luck had not lately seemed to be the order of the day.

"I am beginning to be just like Michael," she reproved herself severely when she reached this point in her meditations. It was fortunate that she did not speak aloud for there was the old gardener himself, just behind her.

She thought that he had come to bid her stop working but, instead, he stood leaning on his hoe, saying nothing. But he was there with something to say, that was evident, for presently, having shifted his feet once or twice and cleared his throat, he was able to begin.

"Miss Betsey," he said slowly, "you don't believe in bad spirits, do you, the kind that bring ill luck to people that deserve only the best and fairest fortune on earth?"

She was quite startled that his thoughts and hers should have been following so closely the same channel, but she would not admit the fact.

"No, Michael, I don't," she answered firmly. "Do you?"

"I'm not sure that I don't, nor yet that I do," he replied doubtfully; "sometimes I think I have let my fancies run away with me my whole life through, so now that I am a foolish old man, I cannot believe my own senses. You don't think for instance—" he lowered his voice almost to a whisper and looked at her keenly through the shadows, "you don't think that there is anything queer amiss up yonder at the old house?"

"Michael!" cried Betsy, too much astonished to keep up her pretense of calmness. "Michael, have you noticed it too? What was it you saw?"

"It was not so much what I saw, for my eyes are dim and old now, it was what I heard. On the very night when Mr. Donald was here and Mr. Reynolds was stricken, that was when I heard. Something moving in the dark, something that muttered to Itself, that stood by the pool for a minute there in the black and white of the moonlight. I heard the water splash like a fish jumping, but I am thinking it was more like a charm for bad luck being dropped in, as such Creatures love to do. I used to think that the bad spell was only on the old house but it is on the water now also, on that pool that lies so deep and quiet and pictures back the stars. If it was running water, now, the spell would carry away, but not with a still basin as that is, the evil lies there so quiet and works and works—"

"Michael," cried Betsey, "you should not believe such things!"

He shook his head.

"I'd like to put it by," he declared, "but how can a man do so? Can you deny there is sorrow come to this house, undeserved and unforeseen? Yes, the curse of ill luck will lie on a house until some one knows how to drive it away. And the best time for lifting such a spell is in the hour before midnight and in the dark of the moon."

Betsey stood up and took her basket.

"I am not going to believe what you say," she insisted stoutly, "and I am going in to see Miss Miranda. You have not told me yet how her father is."

"I had orders not to tell you until I must," he said gently. "He is worse, much worse. The doctor has been here all day and Miss Miranda looks like a ghost."

"Oh," cried Betsey in distress, then added with almost a sob of relief, "Oh, here's David!"

For David, striding out of the shadows, seemed a very comforting presence.

"I nailed them," he announced elegantly the moment he came near. "The examiners were a clever set of fellows, they managed to guess at all the things I knew and to ask me about very little else. I make them my compliments. And now, how are things going?"

He heard the bad news in troubled silence, took up Elizabeth's basket without a word and turned to the house. Poor old Michael stood staring after them, hopeless and distressed, unable to speak.

Miss Miranda stood by the door, talking to the doctor who was just going.

"He is quieter," the doctor was saying, "and the night may pass easily. But if he should be delirious again—"

"I will be here, sir," David announced briefly, at his side.

"You will? Good, you can be of some help if things go badly. And be sure to call me the moment there is any change. If there were only something that would rouse him from that stupor!"

Miss Miranda looked much like a shadow, but she greeted them as cheerily as ever and seemed most eager to know how their affairs had gone during the last three days, and was as happy as they were in the hopeful report of results.

"I was rather worried about David," she admitted, and he confessed cheerfully that he had been much worse than worried about himself.

"At the last minute I began quite to enjoy the excitement of it," he declared, "but I don't care to go through it a second time. I will never cut things quite so close again."

The cottage was to be crowded that night for Elizabeth was to sleep there, upon Miss Miranda's urging it, and David, since there were no more spare beds, undertook to make up a couch for himself on one of the low benches in the workshop. Elizabeth had opportunity, while Miss Miranda had gone to fetch some blankets, of telling David that Michael, too, had been seeing strange things in the garden of the ruined house.

"I can guess what Michael thought if he saw that moving light," the boy observed. "He would have a hundred explanations where we have not been able to find one. When we get some of these other affairs off our minds, we will have to go and watch for it again."

"Y—yes," assented Betsey. She was not entirely sure whether she cared to investigate further.

"There is one thing that I have found out," he went on. "I came across the grounds of the old house this evening while it was still light, to gather up some of the books I used to keep there and that I will not use again. And I found that these last spring storms have weakened and washed out those broken walls worse than ever, so that nothing but a ghost or goblin could walk over them without coming to grief."

Betsey said good night to David, good night to Miss Miranda, tiptoed down the dimly lighted hall and closed the door of her own room.

"You must go to sleep early," Miss Miranda had said. "I know you are tired after your hard three days."

Weary she was, but not sleepy at all. She felt a restless uneasiness nor, try as she would, could she shake off the haunting depression caused by Michael's fantastic notion. She sat by the window, watching big dark clouds creep upward from the horizon and blot out the stars, she wandered about the room, she tried to read, she tried to sleep, but all to no purpose. It was impossible to put out of her mind the seriousness of Mr. Reynolds' illness, nor could she forget Michael's solemn belief that ill luck lay heavy on the place and would not be driven away.

"It's nonsense," she told herself again and again. "Why did I ever listen to him?"

The pressure of excitement and distress became greater and greater instead of less, became almost unendurable. She sat down before Miss Miranda's desk and lifted her hand to the key of the toy-cupboard How often she had read in fairy stories of how the heroine of the tale, when in complete despair, would break the magic nut, uncover the enchanted box for a charm to bring help in time of need. She felt as though it were much the same thing she was doing when she opened the doors of the toy cupboard.

One after another she took down the treasures and set them before her, the silver Saint Christopher, the little jade tree, the bowls and cups, the ornaments and carvings. She tried to recollect the stories she had heard but a few days ago, the gay adventures, the odd, absorbing tales. Yet she came wandering back to the two of which she had heard first, the silver saint and the little tree. They seemed to be more closely bound up with her daily life, with Michael's superstition and with that steadfast purpose that dwelt in the Reynolds' blood. From the two friends who built their clipper ship in the face of all opposition down to Miss Miranda and her father, all were willing to sacrifice so much and work so untiringly to put into reality the substance of a dream. She set the tree on the shelf again and in doing so brushed Saint Christopher to the ground. Poor Michael, what strange ideas had taken possession of his faithful old Irish soul!

"That pool that lies so deep and quiet and pictures back the stars. If it was running water, now!"

Why did his rambling, senseless talk keep running through her head? Little by little, however, calm and comfort seemed to come back to her and at last, so late did she sit before the toy cupboard that drowsiness came from mere force of habit and she got up and stumbled to her bed.

She slept soundly, but for a very little time, awakening with a start. The rising clouds had brought high winds with them, winds that were blustering about the corners of the little house and blowing sticks and broken boughs across the steep roof above her head. Starting up with all sleepiness vanished, she sat staring into the dark. There was a sound above the others that she did not quite recognize, a sound like a door banging or—no—it was the slamming of a gate. Again and again she heard it, an unlocked gate swinging in the wild night wind. There was none near enough for her to hear so plainly save the one in the high garden wall.

Then suddenly there came into her mind, not gradually as answers to puzzles often come, but all at once, full, clear and plain, the truth as to that mystery of the goblin light. Why had she been so dense before, why had she thought of it so late, when real harm might have already come? She fumbled for her clothes in the dark, stumbling here and there in too great haste even to find the lamp; she dressed pell-mell, flung open the door and ran down the stairs. She was quiet in the upper hall, but, in her hurry, had little thought of silence as she unbarred the outer door.

The high, warm wind whirled her halfway across the lawn the moment she stepped off the doorstep. The gate in the wall was swinging open just as she had guessed, the path beyond stretched away like a black tunnel through the trees. She was afraid, she hated to go alone, she felt very small and powerless in all that empty darkness. Why had she not stopped to call David? But no, it would have taken more time than she could afford to lose. She was buffeted by the wind, brushed with ghostly hands by the low-reaching shrubs; she was half sobbing with terror, but nevertheless she ran onward.

CHAPTER XII

THE DARK OF THE MOON

The wide circle of open lawn before the ruined house was less dark than the pathway, but the shadows beneath the trees were inky black and the pines themselves were bowing and thundering in the heavy storm. There was no rain, only the boisterous wind whipping the branches and driving great masses of clouds across the sky with now and then a gleam of stars between. Stars glinted now and again in the pool also, long beams of light in the ruffled water, although, as she came near, there chanced to be quiet for a moment so that she saw reflected the irregular circle of light that Miss Miranda had told her was the Northern Crown.

She stood still by the pool for a long minute, her heart beating very loud, the pulses throbbing in her ears as it does after running. Very keenly she was peering into the dark at the long lines of ruined walls, seeing nothing at first, but by and by catching glimpses of a tiny, moving light. It stopped, vanished, reappeared, and moved on before she could be certain that she really saw it. At last it came nearer, moving along past the door that David had used, slipped over the tumbled wall, even showed double for a second in the shattered old mirror. She was trying to speak, to cry out, but she could not find her voice, could only stare, fascinated, quaking inwardly with the thought that the light, after all, might be something unearthly. But as it progressed farther toward the end of the house where the fire had raged fiercest, the sense of danger brought her to her senses at last.

"Stop," she cried frantically. "It is not safe there. Stop, come back."

She had called a second too late. There was a sound of rending walls and tumbling bricks, a crash, a startled cry and then a groan. She rushed across the grass, could find no place to climb over and ran up and down wildly, seeking a point of vantage where she might scramble across. A new sound caught her attention, for flying feet were coming up the path.

"Oh, David, David is it you?" she cried, in an overwhelming rush of relief. "I can't climb up, I can't reach him."

"You are not to try it, it is not safe," David ordered sternly, setting his foot on the first big block of stone even as he spoke.

"I am going where you go," she replied and evidently he realized it was no time for argument.

"Then this is the best way over. Here, give me your hand, and be careful of that loose beam."

They scrambled over the summit and, amid a shower of sliding bricks, slipped down on the other side. A dark figure lay stretched upon the stones, moving a little and still holding a flickering, lighted candle. It was Michael.

"Yes, Miss Betsey dear," he affirmed cheerfully, when they had at last brought him to recognize who they were, "and I've a broken leg I'm thinking from the way it feels by not having any feeling at all. And will you hold up the candle and see what is running down my face?"

"Oh, Michael, Michael, what were you doing, how could you be so foolish?" Betsey reproached him; "your head is cut and what is running over your face is blood." She began, forthwith, to try to tie it up with her handkerchief.

"Then glory be to all the Saints," was Michael's unexpectedly joyful reply; "there is nothing that will break the charm of ill luck like the letting of blood. It will all go well now."

Betsey looked helplessly at David. Was the poor old man gone out of his wits entirely?

"Don't you know better than to risk your life over such nonsense? Won't you ever learn better, Michael?" David said severely, although the pathetic broken figure on the stones was one to call forth only pity.

"Yes," assented the old Irishman meekly, "I know better and the priest is always telling me so. But yet—when there's trouble to them you love and seemingly no way out of it, why, you look back at the old fancies and wonder if they were not true after all, and you feel the need to try this thing or to try that thing, just in case there might be help in it."

"And what were you doing here?" David asked.

"It is on this house that the ill luck lies, for it was in its burning that the evil fortune began and it is only through its building up again that happiness can come back to Miss Miranda. And so—and so—just to make the luck change, it is the old way to take a candle in your hand and to walk through every part of the house saying spells as you go. And the last of the spells must be said in the hour before midnight in the dark of the moon. But Miss Betsey stopped me," he concluded regretfully. "This was to be the last night, yet I did not get the whole of the way."

"She came just in time," David corrected him. "The walls beyond here are weaker even than these, and high enough to bury you completely if they should fall. I was awake and heard the gate swinging, and I was trying to think how it came to be open, but it was Betsey that was quick enough to understand in time. When she ran down the stairs I got up to follow her, yet I really did not guess what was happening until I heard you fall. You must thank her that you are still alive."

"But if the bad luck still holds," protested Michael pitifully, "then it will be all to do over again!"

He was silent as though gathering strength for further speech and then began once more.

"And I must tell you that what has been going amiss is, the whole of it, through fault of mine. There was a day, it was before you ever came to the cottage, when Mr. Donald was last here that—that—" His voice faltered, perhaps through weakness, perhaps through reluctance to go on, but he drew a breath and continued bravely. "That very morning, when I was getting my breakfast I spilled the salt dish and I thought to myself, 'Michael Martin, you will be losing your temper with some one this day.' But who was there for me to quarrel with except Miss Miranda and her father and the good Saints know I could never be vexed with them. So I went about my work and thought no more about it.

THE POOL OF STARS

"But that afternoon I went over to the old house, it was late winter still and I was wishing to gather some pine cones for Miss Miranda's hearth, and, for all the cold, I sat down on a stone to smoke a pipe and think about the old times and how happy we all were before the fire came. And there was Mr. Donald, walking about the broken walls, peering here and peering there, but not stepping within for he is of the sort that are always careful of the safety of their precious skins."

He stopped again to rest his trembling voice.

"Don't try to tell us, Michael, if it is so hard," Elizabeth said.

"I must tell you, Miss Betsey," he replied, "I have hid it in my heart too long. He says to me, 'I am just looking to see where the fire really started, it seems that it must have been at this end where the workshop stood.' I says 'Yes, sir,' not being wishful to have any talk with him. And after a little he says again, 'It was a beautiful old place. I can see plainly why Miranda longs for it and cannot be happy where she is.' And this time I says nothing but puffs away at my pipe. It roused my anger, some way, to see him peering about, though I am a slow-witted fellow and had no guess at what he was looking for. At last he speaks once more. 'Why don't they build it up again, Michael?' he says. 'They could if they weren't such a careless impractical pair. They should be living here again, I have no patience with them.' Then my wrath boils up in me and I tells him what I thinks. 'You have no patience, have you,' says I, 'with them that took you in and cared for you and bore with those ways you have that no one likes. You're prosperous yourself through their help, if you want them to rebuild their house why don't you give them aid in doing it? Miss Miranda toils and saves and has her garden and her ducks and anything she can think of to make things go forward, so that her father will have what he needs for his work.' All of that I says to him and I wish the Saints had struck me dumb before I spoke.

"'She works so that her father may have what he needs?' he repeats. 'So that is how things stand, just as I had been suspecting. Thank you, Michael, that is all I wanted to know,' he says and goes, leaving me gaping after him as he walks away over the snow. I did not know even then what use he was to make of what I had told him, but I saw well enough that I had done harm. And so I have been doing all I could to make amends," he ended sadly; "I have watched over the house that he should never come near with Miss Miranda not there, though I guessed but little what it was he would do. And when it seemed of no use and I felt helpless and afraid, thinking of the mischief I had done, I have turned to trying to drive away the ill luck in the old fashion, with spells and charms, just—just because there might be something in them after all."

He ceased speaking and closed his eyes, worn out by the effort of confession.

"He used to watch by the garden gate long before Miss Miranda's cousin ever showed himself," was Betsey's whispered comment to David. "He was sitting there on the bench in the dark, that night we sat by the pool and Miss Miranda told us the story of the green jade tree. He was probably watching on the very evening that Donald Reynolds finally came."

"Yes," David reminded her bitterly, "and slipped away on a chase after a will-o'-the-wisp, lit his candle and came up here to this place when he might have been of some real use at home. He even brought us there after him, though he did not know it, just at the time when the man he dreaded had really come. If he had only been sensible—"

"Don't let him think of that," said Betsey. "Yes, he went at just the wrong minute but he must be kept from remembering it."

Michael must have suspected that their whispered discussion concerned the truth of his strange notions.

"Maybe I was wrong," he said miserably, "but did not my own eyes see Something stand there by the pool, did not my ears hear a splash in the water that boded no good. If it had only been running water—"

Betsey felt David start suddenly in the dark.

"Say that again, Michael," he ordered breathlessly.

The old Irishman repeated the words faithfully, even to the groan at the end of them. David's excitement was rapidly communicating itself to Betsey.

"That was on the night Miss Miranda's father was taken ill," she said, although of this explanation there was no need.

"I know, I know," the boy returned quickly, "but wasn't Mr. Reynolds in his shop all the rest of the evening? That is what has puzzled me."

"I looked in once and he was gone," she answered, "but it was for such a little while that I never thought of it again. Oh, if we should find what is lost, at last!"

David was already on his feet, peering over the stone wall toward the pool.

"We should try to get Michael home first," Betsey objected, seeing already what was in his mind.

"No, no," the Irishman insisted, having only a vague notion of what they were about, but feeling excitement in the air. "You shall not move me one inch if there is aught to do first that may help Miss Miranda."

"You must lie very still," warned Betsey.

"Indeed and I will," promised Michael obediently, "but—what is it you are going to do, you two?"

They did not stop to explain, so great was their haste. They went clambering over the wall again, and tumbled down the other side upon the grass. The wind, from which they had been sheltered below, caught them again as they ran to the pool. They knelt down at opposite sides of the shallow curve and plunged their arms, shoulder deep, into the tossing water.

"I have found something," exclaimed Betsey almost immediately; "it feels like thin metal blades set in a ring."

She drew her prize, dripping, from the basin and held it up. As she sat back on her heels the wind loosened her hair and flung its dark mass over her shoulder. David, unable to see, took the object in his hand and felt of it carefully.

"That is certainly the missing valve," he pronounced, "so we know now that we are right. The other parts were two steel tubes, about as long as my hand. Those will not be so easy to find. They may have rolled away to the deep end."

No amount of fumbling on the bottom revealed anything further except that Betsey, lifting a stone, grasped a frog that was beneath it and almost tumbled into the water with the dreadful start its slippery little body caused her. She sat up, panting, and attempted to wring out her wet sleeve.

"What if we could not find them after all," she lamented. "Mr. Reynolds must have meant that no one, not even himself, should ever have them again."

But David was not willing to give up so easily.

"It is like a needle in a haystack," he admitted, "but even such things have been found."

He poised himself at the edge of the basin, then slid into the water with the clean straight dive of an expert swimmer. Once he went down, and twice, and came up empty handed. The third time he was gone so long that the water quieted and the reflected stars shone once more in their places. Betsey, leaning over to watch in an agony of apprehension, felt her tired spirit completely give way.

"Oh, David," she wailed, although under her breath, "don't be drowned and leave me alone in the dark."

As though in answer to her words a widening circle suddenly appeared on the surface and David's head rose at the center of the pool. He gasped and spluttered and shook the water from his eyes.

"I have them," he announced joyfully, "one in each hand. Now we have found them all."

He came clambering out on the edge of the basin, the water pouring from him in streams, his red head sleek and shining.

"I got a little short of breath that last time," he admitted. "I kept touching the things and they kept rolling away, I thought I would never get them in my hands. They would have rusted to bits in a little longer; we have not found them at all too soon."

THE POOL OF STARS

Michael's wits seemed to be wandering a little when they returned to him, nor did he appear to understand very clearly the account that, both speaking excitedly, they poured into his ears.

"Of course, of course," he kept repeating a little impatiently, "did I not tell you that the secret of the ill luck charm lay in the pool of stars?"

"You did, Michael," Betsey agreed soothingly at last, "but you see we did not quite understand."

"And now," said David, getting up, "I am going back to the cottage to telephone for the doctor and to bring help to carry Michael home. It will not be long."

Betsey sat very quiet after he had gone. The wind whooped and whirled overhead, bowing the trees and beating back and forth the branches of the vines and shrubs. All at once she began to hear a strange cracking, a grating of stones and the snapping of ivy stems, the crushing of bushes, then an appalling rumble that grew to a deafening crash of falling stone. Even in the sheltered corner where they were, the ground rocked and a cloud of gritty dust blew in upon them, almost choking them both. Michael, startled, actually managed to raise himself on his elbow.

"What was that?" he asked.

"The wind has carried down the last walls that were standing in the south wing," she replied. "David said that they have been crumbling for years and that lately, with feet going back and forth over them, they have grown more and more ready to fall. I am glad you did not go farther, you might have been hurt worse than this."

The old man's brain seemed to have been aroused by the shock into a moment of absolute clearness.

"I should have been buried entirely, I am thinking," he remarked, "and there would have been an end to an old fool and his whims and fancies. I sought to set things right in my own way and have done nothing but harm, while it is you and Mr. David have found out all the trouble by your plain good sense and loyal friendship, and will know how to mend what has gone amiss. It is your standing so firm by Miss Miranda that has made things go well again."

"But it was you who told me to stand by her," Betsey reminded him comfortingly. "I would never have dreamed that I could help her if you had not told me so."

He was quiet a little but presently spoke again.

"When they come to carry me home it may be the pain of lifting me over the wall will disorder my wits once more. So I should tell you what was to be a secret, that Mr. Ted comes home to-day. That was why I was so anxious the bad luck should be gone on this very night, and thanks to you, it is. He was not quite certain of the time and did not wish to disappoint his sister, so it was to old Michael he sent the message to be on the watch for him. We were always great friends, Mr. Ted and me, and to think that the blessed Saint Christopher has brought him home safe at last."

He must have made an effort to tell this, feeling that his senses were once more slipping from him for almost immediately he went off again into confused muttering.

"He saved my life," he said once, more clearly, "he saved my sheep, him and those great beautiful white dogs, but—" the thread of consciousness had snapped again—"they were always the hunters, those greyhounds of the King of Connemara; though they lived a thousand years ago you can hear their cry over the hills to this day!"

It was, to Betsey, a moment of great relief, when she heard feet upon the grassy pathway, saw the gleam of lanterns through the rifts in the broken walls and knew that help had come. Later, however, there was a very hard hour at the old man's tiny cottage when the doctor attended to his broken leg and the gash in his head.

"He will get through all right," was the cheerful assurance given when the affair was over. "I have attended Michael before, he gets himself into many scrapes but he always comes out of them."

The nurse had come down to give assistance, but she and the doctor were both needed at Mr. Reynolds' bedside. When questioned about Miss Miranda's father, the doctor merely shook his head.

They went away, leaving Betsey to watch Michael alone, since David also had betaken himself to the cottage. She sat for hour after long hour

THE POOL OF STARS

until it was beginning to be morning, as she could see from her place by the bed near the tiny window. The birds were singing; perhaps it was that same thrush that had greeted her before, that was swinging from the drooping elm tree and calling its welcome to the dawn. Michael was sleeping peacefully, she felt very weary herself as she sat there watching the gray light turn slowly to bright day. A step fell on the threshold, a heavy step that could be none other than Mrs. Bassett's.

"These are the strangest doings that ever I heard of," she exclaimed as she came in, taking off her coat and putting on her apron almost with the same motion. "To think that I slept through it all and never knew a thing until that boy, tinkering in the workshop before it was light, happened to wake me. I've got the breakfast ready up there at Miss Miranda's, and set everything to rights and now I am just going to stay here while you go back and get some sleep. What a time you have had, poor dear! They say Mr. Reynolds has got through the night a little better than they hoped, though there is still nothing that will rouse him from that stupor."

The sun was really up and shining as Betsey passed through the garden toward the cottage. The world was very clean and glittering and very still, with only the old cock strutting across the poultry yard and lifting his voice in a loud, full crow that sounded far through the quiet of the dawn. It was a pleasant, homely, familiar sound after the strange adventures and unrealities of the night. Betsey began to wonder if it had not indeed been all a dream and she would not presently discover that she had dropped asleep before the toy-cupboard, the tree of jade or the silver Saint Christopher in her hand.

Black Dick, strutting and fluttering before the workshop, seemed to be telling her, before she could run across the grass to the door, that something of great moment was going on inside. David was busy with his back toward her, a very jubilant and excited David, still in the damp, bedraggled clothes of last night's adventures, but whistling gayly and handling wrench and hammer as though life itself depended on his speed. He looked at her over his shoulder, smiling his widest and happiest smile.

"Don't go," he said, breathless and eager, "don't go. Something—something is just going to happen!"

There was the snapping of a switch and the slow creak of a lever that had not recently been moved. Then followed a faint and rising hum, a whir of wheels grew louder and deeper, that filled the death-like silence of the room with gay song, that sounded over the garden and through the house, that reached the ears of the invalid upstairs and made him stir and smile and open his eyes.

Betsey listened enthralled, too filled with breathless delight to heed any other sound. Yet the gate from the lane was flung hastily and noisily open and a man in uniform came striding up the path. She did not even heed when Dick, with joyous cawing, spread wide black wings to fly to the stranger's shoulder, she only looked up, startled, to see him standing in the inner hallway beyond the workshop door. There was something of Miss Miranda in his bearing, something of her spirit in his dancing eyes. And his voice, somehow, had a faint ring of her father's when he called up the stair, the same familiar call, but with no note of worried helplessness like Mr. Reynolds', only the ringing tidings of a brother's long-desired homecoming—

"Miranda, oh, Miranda."

CONCLUSION

The summer had slipped away, the garden on the hillside was golden instead of green and old white Dobbin was plowing for autumn's sowing instead of spring's. Michael, possessed still of a slight limp and a scar on his seamed forehead, but hale and lusty as before, dug among the potatoes and had no one to tempt him from his habitual silence. Miss Miranda was busy elsewhere and as for Elizabeth and David, the garden and the yellow fields knew them no more.

Betsey's father had come home and had set up his housekeeping in the college town so that he and his daughter need not be separated again. Aunt Susan also had returned, laden with souvenirs, curios, new clothes, and glorious accounts of what she had seen. The descriptions, however, like her collection of photographs, were apt to become a little jumbled when brought out for exhibition, so that Betsey was never really quite certain whether Bermuda was chiefly delightful for its mountain ranges or its shopping, or whether Lake Louise, a marvel of scenic wonder as she understood, was situated in the Canadian Rockies or the Garden of the Gods. As a result she could not feel any sharp or definite regret for what she had missed.

The completed invention had brought Miss Miranda's father both fame and fortune, even as his scientist friend had prophesied, and what was better, had won him back to health. The first result of its success was that the ruined walls of the old house had vanished and the big, gray, beautiful building was going up again under the hands of an army of workmen. Mr. Reynolds could be seen upon the lawn, superintending mildly with Miss Miranda at his side, a very changed and happy Miss Miranda who seemed to love watching one stone replaced above another as though each were a miracle. When Elizabeth and David should come back for the first vacation of their college year, the house would be under roof at least, so that warm red tiles and sharp gable-lines would be reflected in the pool on the lawn. There would be scarlet leaves floating in the water then, and dry, brown grass nodding at the edge and, on quiet evenings, there would rock upon the ripples the shining stars of Orion or the laughing Pleiades.

That time, however, was still distant, for Betsey and David were entering, this morning, on their first day of college. They had journeyed from Harwood and came up from the station together, but now stood near the great gray arch that led to the main campus, at the place where they must part. The Scientific School, where David was to enter, stood just across the road, showing a brick-columned entrance-way with heavy iron gates and a hurrying throng passing out and in. The two had been discussing the future year most earnestly when they set out, but the talk had languished and they had fallen quite silent now. Hundreds of people, it seemed, were hastening past them, all young, all eager, all absorbed in their varied errands.

"I dread a little," Betsey confessed at last; "it is so new and strange and different. I wanted so much to come here, but now, just at the last minute, I would be glad to go home again."

David nodded.

"I feel the same way," he agreed. "But I think anything big enough to be worth while is bound to be dreaded a little too. The feeling won't last long. Well, the bell is ringing, we must go on, I think."

They said good-by and turned to go in their opposite directions. Beyond the vine-covered arch a great bell was swinging in one of those same towers that they had watched across the valley, a silvery, sweet-voiced bell, for all the greatness of its sound. Betsey walked forward, surrounded more and more by hurrying companions, a few of them girls from her school whom she knew, many, many of them strangers, but all looking as though they might some day be friends. It was a close-pressing throng as she came to the entrance of the main building where she must go in, so that she had to mount slowly, step by step, to the door. She could look back, down the straight walk, under the arch, through the great gate opposite to where, far beyond, a similar group was pressing into a similar doorway. For a fleeting second she felt a little lonely, a little homesick, before such sensations were carried away in the rush of excited thought of all that was in store for her. She was glad that she could still see David's red head from afar and that it was the last thing of which she caught a glimpse, just as the hastening crowd swept her across the threshold and into a new world.

THE END

CPSIA information can be obtained
at www.ICGtesting.com
Printed in the USA
LVHW081603210720
661230LV00027B/1132